CRA

✔ **KT-425-906**

How to Talk About

Books You Haven't Read

How to Talk About
Books You Haven't Read

PIERRE BAYARD

Translated from the French
by Jeffrey Mehlman

Granta Books
London

Granta Publications, 12–14 Addison Avenue, London W11 4QR

First published in Great Britain by Granta Books 2008
First published in the United States in 2007 by Bloomsbury

English translation copyright © 2007 by Jeffrey Mehlman

Copyright © 2007 Les Editions de Minuit
Originally published in French as
Comment parler des livres que l'on n'a pas lus?

A CIP catalogue record for this book is
available from the British Library.

1 3 5 7 9 10 8 6 4 2

Printed and bound in Great Britain by
William Clowes Ltd, Beccles, Suffolk

028

X 000.000. 031 .3408

I never read a book I must review; it prejudices you so.

—OSCAR WILDE

Contents

(in which the reader will see, as demonstrated by a character of Musil's, that reading any particular book is a waste of time compared to keeping our perspective about books overall)

(in which we see, along with Valéry, that it is enough to have skimmed a book to be able to write an article about it, and that with certain books it might even be inappropriate to do otherwise)

(in which Umberto Eco shows that it is wholly unnecessary to have held a book in your hand to be able to speak about it in detail, as long as you listen to and read what others say about it)

List of Abbreviations

Op. cit.	work cited
Ibid.	ibidem
UB	book unknown to me
SB	book I have skimmed
HB	book I have heard about
FB	book I have forgotten
++	extremely positive opinion
+	positive opinion
–	negative opinion
– –	extremely negative opinion

Preface

BORN INTO A MILIEU where reading was rare, deriving little pleasure from the activity, and lacking in any case the time to devote myself to it, I have often found myself in the delicate situation of having to express my thoughts on books I haven't read.

Because I teach literature at the university level, there is, in fact, no way to avoid commenting on books that most of the time I haven't even opened. It's true that this is also the case for the majority of my students, but if even one of them has read the text I'm discussing, there is a risk that at any moment my class will be disrupted and I will find myself humiliated.

In addition, I am regularly called on to discuss publications in my books and articles, since these for the most part concern the books and articles of others. This exercise is even more problematic, since unlike spoken statements—which can include imprecisions without consequence—written commentaries leave traces and can be verified.

As a result of such all-too-familiar situations, I believe I am well positioned, if not to offer any real lesson on the subject, at least to convey a deeper understanding of the non-reader's experience and to undertake a meditation on this forbidden subject.

∾

It is unsurprising that so few texts extol the virtues of non-reading. Indeed, to describe your experience in this area, as I will attempt here, demands a certain courage, for doing so clashes inevitably with a whole series of internalized constraints. Three of these, at least, are crucial.

The first of these constraints might be called the obligation to read. We still live in a society, on the decline though it may be, where reading remains the object of a kind of worship. This worship applies particularly to a number of canonical texts—the list varies according to the circles you move in—which it is practically forbidden not to have read if you want to be taken seriously.

The second constraint, similar to the first but nonetheless distinct, might be called the obligation to read thoroughly. If it's frowned upon not to read, it's almost as bad to read quickly or to skim, and especially to say so. For example, it's virtually unthinkable for literary intellectuals to acknowledge that they have flipped through Proust's work without having read it in its entirety—though this is certainly the case for most of them.

The third constraint concerns the way we discuss books. There is a tacit understanding in our culture that one must read a book in order to talk about it with any precision. In my experience, however, it's totally possible to carry on an

engaging conversation about a book you haven't read—
including, and perhaps especially, with someone else who
hasn't read it either.

Moreover, as I will argue, it is sometimes easier to do jus-
tice to a book if you haven't read it in its entirety—or even
opened it. Throughout this book, I will insist on the risks of
reading—so frequently underestimated—for anyone who in-
tends to talk about books, and even more so for those who
plan to review them.

∼

The effect of this repressive system of obligations and prohi-
bitions has been to generate a widespread hypocrisy on the
subject of books that we actually *have* read. I know few areas
of private life, with the exception of finance and sex, in
which it's as difficult to obtain accurate information.

Among specialists, mendacity is the rule, and we tend to lie
in proportion to the significance of the book under consideration. Although I've read relatively little myself, I'm familiar
enough with certain books—here, again, I'm thinking of
Proust—to be able to evaluate whether my colleagues are
telling the truth when they talk about his work, and to know
that in fact, they rarely are.

These lies we tell to others are first and foremost lies we
tell ourselves, for we have trouble acknowledging even to
ourselves that we haven't read the books that are deemed essential. And here, just as in so many other domains of life, we
show an astonishing ability to reconstruct the past to better
conform to our wishes.

Our propensity to lie when we talk about books is a logical consequence of the stigma attached to non-reading, which in turn arises from a whole network of anxieties rooted (no doubt) in early childhood. If we wish, then, to learn how to emerge unscathed from conversations about books we haven't read, it will be necessary to analyze the unconscious guilt that an admission of non-reading elicits. It is to help assuage such guilt, at least in part, that is the goal of this book.

~

It is all the more difficult to reflect on unread books and the discussions they engender because the concept of non-reading is itself unclear, and so it is often hard to know whether we're lying or not when we say that we've read a book. The very question implies that we can draw a clear line between reading and not reading, while in fact many of the ways we encounter texts sit somewhere between the two.

Between a book we've read closely and a book we've never even heard of, there is a whole range of gradations that deserve our attention. In the case of books we have supposedly read, we must consider just what is meant by *reading*, a term that can refer to a variety of practices. Conversely, many books that by all appearances we haven't read exert an influence on us nevertheless, as their reputations spread through society.

The uncertainty of the border between reading and not reading will lead me to reflect more generally on the ways we interact with books. Thus my inquiry will not be limited to developing techniques for escaping awkward literary confrontations. By analyzing these situations, I will also attempt to articulate a genuine theory of reading—one that dispenses with our image of it as a simple, seamless process and, instead, embraces all its fault lines, deficiencies, and approximations.

~

These remarks bring us logically to the organization of this book. I will begin in the first section by describing the principal kinds of non-reading—which, as we will see, goes far beyond the act of leaving a book unopened. To varying degrees, books we've skimmed, books we've heard about, and books we have forgotten also fall into the rich category that is non-reading.

A second section will be devoted to analyzing concrete situations in which we might find ourselves talking about books we haven't read. Life, in its cruelty, presents us with a plethora of such circumstances, and it is beyond the scope of this project to enumerate them all. But a few significant examples—sometimes borrowed, in disguised form, from my own experience—may allow us to identify some patterns that I will draw on in advancing my argument.

The third and most important section is the one that motivated me to write this book. It consists of a series of simple recommendations gathered over a lifetime of non-reading. This advice is intended to help anyone who encounters one of these social dilemmas to resolve it as well as possible, and even to benefit from the situation, while also permitting him or her to reflect deeply on the act of reading.

~

These opening remarks are intended not only to explain the general structure of this book, but also to remind us of the peculiar relation to truth that infuses all our traditional ways of referring to books. To get to the heart of things, I believe we must significantly modify how we talk about books, even the specific words we use to describe them.

In keeping with my general thesis, which posits that the notion of the book-that-has-been-read is ambiguous, from this point forward I will indicate the extent of my personal knowledge of each book I cite, via a system of abbreviations.[1] This series of indications, which will be clarified as we go, is intended to complete those that traditionally appear in foot-notes, and that are used to designate the books the author theoretically has read (*op. cit., ibid.*, etc.). In fact, as I will re-veal through my own case, authors often refer to books of which we have only scanty knowledge, and so I will attempt to break with the misrepresentation of reading by specifying exactly what I know of each book.

I will complement this first series of indications with a second series conveying my opinion of the books being cited, whether or not they have ever passed through my hands.[2] Since I will argue that evaluating a book does not

---

1. The four abbreviations used will be explained in the first four chapters. UB designates books unknown to me; SB, books I have skimmed; HB, books I have heard of; FB, books I have forgotten (see the list of abbreviations). These abbre-viations are not mutually exclusive. An indication is given for every book title, and only at its first mention.
2. The abbreviations used are ++ (extremely positive opinion), + (positive opinion), − (negative opinion), and −− (extremely negative opinion). See the list of abbreviations.

require having read it, there is, after all, no reason for me to refrain from passing judgment on whatever works I come across, even if I have never heard of them before.[3]

This new system of notations—which I hope will one day be widely adopted—is intended as a ongoing reminder that our relation to books is not the continuous and homogeneous process that certain critics would have us imagine, nor the site of some transparent self-knowledge. Our relation to books is a shadowy space haunted by the ghosts of memory, and the real value of books lies in their ability to conjure these specters.

---

3. It will be observed that this system of notations is valuable as well for its omissions, specifically RB (book that has been read) and NRB (book that has not been read), the very notations one might have expected, which will never be used. It is precisely in opposition to this kind of artificial distinction that the book is organized, a distinction conveying an image of reading that makes it hard to think about the way we actually experience it.

Ways of Not Reading

I

Books You Don't Know

(in which the reader will see, as demonstrated by
a character of Musil's, that reading any particular
book is a waste of time compared to keeping
our perspective about books overall)

THERE IS MORE THAN one way not to read, the most radical
of which is not to open a book at all. For any given reader,
however dedicated he might be, such total abstention necessarily holds true for virtually everything that has been published, and thus in fact this constitutes our primary way of
relating to books. We must not forget that even a prodigious
reader never has access to more than an infinitesimal fraction
of the books that exist. As a result, unless he abstains defini-
tively from all conversation and all writing, he will find himself forever obliged to express his thoughts on books he hasn't
read.

If we take this attitude to the extreme, we arrive at the case
of the absolute non-reader, who never opens a book and yet
knows them and talks about them without hesitation. Such is

the case of the librarian in *The Man Without Qualities*,[1] a secondary character in Musil's novel, but one whose radical position and courage in defending it make him essential to our argument.

~

Musil's novel takes place at the beginning of the last century in a country called Kakania, a parody of the Austro-Hungarian Empire. A patriotic movement, known as Parallel Action, has been founded to organize a lavish celebration of the upcoming anniversary of the emperor's reign, a celebration that is intended to serve as a redemptive example for the rest of the world.

The leaders of Parallel Action, whom Musil depicts as so many ridiculous marionettes, are thus all in search of a "redemptive idea," which they evoke endlessly yet in the vaguest of terms—for indeed, they have neither the slightest inkling of what the idea might be nor how it might perform its redemptive function beyond their country's borders.

Among the movement's leaders, one of the most ridiculous is General Stumm (which means "mute" in German). Stumm is determined to discover the redemptive idea before the others as an offering to the woman he loves—Diotima, who is also prominent within Parallel Action:

"You remember, don't you," he said, "that I'd made up my mind to find that great redeeming idea Diotima wants and lay it at her feet. It turns out that there are

1. SB and HB++.

lots of great ideas, but only one of them can be the greatest—that's only logical, isn't it?—so it's a matter of putting them in order."[2]

The general, a man of little experience with ideas and their manipulation, never mind methods for developing new ones, decides to go to the imperial library—that wellspring of fresh thoughts—to "become informed about the resources of the adversary" and to discover the "redemptive idea" with utmost efficiency.

∼

The visit to the library plunges this man of limited familiarity with books into profound anguish. As a military officer, he is used to being in a position of dominance, yet here he finds himself confronted with a form of knowledge that offers him no landmarks, nothing to hold on to:

> "We marched down the ranks in that colossal store house of books, and I don't mind telling you I was not particularly overwhelmed; those rows of books are not particularly worse than a garrison on parade. Still, after a while I couldn't help starting to do some figuring in my head, and I got an unexpected answer. You see, I had been thinking that if I read a book a day, it would naturally be

---

2. Robert Musil, *The Man Without Qualities*, vol. 1, translated by Sophie Wilkins (New York: Knopf, 1995), p. 500. In this quotation as in the others, Stumm is speaking to his friend Ulrich.

exhausting, but I would be bound to get to the end some-
time and then, even if I had to skip a few, I could claim a
certain position in the world of the intellect. But what do
you suppose the librarian said to me, as we walked on and
on, without an end in sight, and I asked him how many
books they had in this crazy library? Three and a half mil-
lion, he tells me. We had just got to the seven hundred
thousands or so, but I kept on doing these figures in my
head; I'll spare you the details, but I checked it out later
in the office, with pencil and paper: it would take me ten
thousand years to carry out my plan."[3]

This encounter with the infinity of available books offers
a certain encouragement not to read at all. Faced with a
quantity of books so vast that nearly all of them must remain
unknown, how can we escape the conclusion that even a lifetime of reading is utterly in vain?

Reading is first and foremost non-reading. Even in the
case of the most passionate lifelong readers, the act of picking
up and opening a book masks the countergesture that occurs
at the same time: the involuntary act of *not* picking up and *not*
opening all the other books in the universe.

∽

If *The Man Without Qualities* brings up the problem of how
cultural literacy intersects with the infinite, it also presents a

---

3. Ibid., pp. 500–501.

possible solution, one adopted by the librarian helping General Stumm. This librarian has found a way to orient himself among the millions of volumes in his library, if not among all the books in the world. His technique is extraordinary in its simplicity:

> "When I didn't let go of him he suddenly pulled himself up, rearing up in those wobbly pants of his, and said in a slow, very emphatic way, as though the time had come to give away the ultimate secret: 'General,' he said, 'if you want to know how I know about every book here, I can tell you! Because I never read any of them.' "[4]

The general is astonished by this unusual librarian, who vigilantly avoids reading not for any want of culture, but, on the contrary, in order to better know his books:

> "It was almost too much, I tell you! But when he saw how stunned I was, he explained himself. 'The secret of a good librarian is that he never reads anything more of the literature in his charge than the titles and the table of contents. Anyone who lets himself go and starts reading a book is lost as a librarian,' he explained. 'He's bound to lose perspective.'
>
> 'So,' I said, trying to catch my breath, 'you never read a single book?'
>
> 'Never. Only the catalogs.'

---

4. Ibid., p. 503.

'But aren't you a Ph.D.?'

'Certainly I am. I teach at the university, as a special lecturer in Library Science. Library Science is a special field leading to a degree, you know," he explained. "How many systems do you suppose there are, General, for the arrangement and preservation of books, cataloging of titles, correcting misprints and misinformation on title pages, and the like?' "[5]

Musil's librarian thus keeps himself from entering into the books under his care, but he is far from indifferent or hostile toward them, as one might suppose. On the contrary, it is his love of books—of *all* books—that incites him to remain prudently on their periphery, for fear that too pronounced an interest in one of them might cause him to neglect the others.

∼

To me, the wisdom of Musil's librarian lies in this idea of maintaining perspective. What he says about libraries, indeed, is probably true of cultural literacy in general: he who pokes his nose into a book is abandoning true cultivation, and perhaps even reading itself. For there is necessarily a choice to be made, given the number of books in existence, between the overall view and each individual book, and all reading is a squandering of energy in the difficult and time-consuming attempt to master the whole.

---

5. Ibid.

The wisdom of this position lies first of all in the importance it accords to totality, in its suggestion that to be truly cultured, we should tend toward exhaustiveness rather than the accumulation of isolated bits of knowledge. Moreover, the search for totality changes how we look at each book, allowing us to move beyond its individuality to the relations it enjoys with others.

These are the relations that a true reader should attempt to grasp, as Musil's librarian well understands. As a result, like many of his colleagues, he is less interested in books than in books about books:

> "I went on a little longer about needing a kind of timetable that would enable me to make connections among all kinds of ideas in every direction—at which point he turns so polite it's absolutely unholy, and offers to take me into the catalog room and let me do my own searching, even though it's against the rules, because it's only for the use of the librarians. So I actually found myself inside the holy of holies. It felt like being inside an enormous brain. Imagine being totally surrounded by those shelves, full of books in their compartments, ladders all over the place, all those book stands and library tables piled high with catalogs and bibliographies, the concentrate of all knowledge, don't you know, and not one sensible book to read, only books about books."[6]

---

6. Ibid., p. 502.

Rather than any particular book, it is indeed these connections and correlations that should be the focus of the cultivated individual, much as a railroad switchman should focus on the relations between trains—that is, their crossings and transfers—rather than the contents of any specific convoy. And Musil's image of the brain powerfully underscores this theory that relations among ideas are far more important than the ideas themselves.

You could quibble with the librarian's claim not to read any books, since he takes a close interest in the books about books known as catalogs. But these have a rather particular status and in fact amount to no more than lists. They are also a visual manifestation of the relations among books—relations that should be of keen interest to anyone who truly cares about books, who loves them enough to want to master all of them at once.

∾

The idea of perspective so central to the librarian's reasoning has considerable bearing for us on the practical level. It is an intuitive grasp of this same concept that allows certain privileged individuals to escape unharmed from situations in which they might otherwise be accused of being flagrantly culturally deficient.

As cultivated people know (and, to their misfortune, uncultivated people do not), culture is above all a matter of *orientation*. Being cultivated is a matter not of having read any book in particular, but of being able to find your bearings within books as a system, which requires you to know that they form a system and to be able to locate each element in relation to the others. The interior of the book is less important than its exterior, or, if you prefer, the interior of the book *is* its exterior, since what counts in a book is the books alongside it.

It is, then, hardly important if a cultivated person hasn't read a given book, for though he has no exact knowledge of its *content*, he may still know its *location*, or in other words how it is situated in relation to other books. This distinction between the content of a book and its location is fundamental, for it is this that allows those unintimidated by culture to speak without trouble on any subject.

For instance, I've never "read" Joyce's *Ulysses*,[7] and it's quite plausible that I never will. The "content" of the book is thus largely foreign to me—its content, but not its location. Of course, the content of a book *is* in large part its location. This means that I feel perfectly comfortable when *Ulysses* comes up in conversation, because I can situate it with relative precision in relation to other books. I know, for example, that it is a retelling of the *Odyssey*,[8] that its narration takes the form of a stream of consciousness, that its action unfolds in Dublin in the course of a single day, etc. And as a result, I often find myself alluding to Joyce without the slightest anxiety.

Even better, as we shall see in analyzing the power relations behind how we talk about reading, I am able to allude to my non-reading of Joyce without any shame. My intellectual library, like every library, is composed of gaps and blanks, but

7. HB++.
8. SB and HB++.

in reality this presents no real problem: it is sufficiently well stocked for any particular lacuna to be all but invisible.

Most statements about a book are not about the book itself, despite appearances, but about the larger set of books on which our culture depends at that moment. It is that set, which I shall henceforth refer to as the *collective library*, that truly matters, since it is our mastery of this collective library that is at stake in all discussions about books. But this mastery is a command of relations, not of any book in isolation, and it easily accommodates ignorance of a large part of the whole.

It can be argued, then, that a book stops being unknown as soon as it enters our perceptual field, and that to know almost nothing about it should be no obstacle to imagining or discussing it. To a cultivated or curious person, even the slightest glance at a book's title or cover calls up a series of images and impressions quick to coalesce into an initial opinion, facilitated by the whole set of books represented in the culture at large. For the non-reader, therefore, even the most fleeting encounter with a book may be the beginning of an authentic personal appropriation, and any unknown book we come across becomes a known book in that instant.

≈

What distinguishes the non-reading of Musil's librarian is that his attitude is not passive, but active. If many cultivated individuals are non-readers, and if, conversely, many non-readers are cultivated individuals, it is because non-reading is not just the absence of reading. It is a genuine activity, one that consists of adopting a stance in relation to the immense tide of books that protects you from drowning. On that basis, it deserves to be defended and even taught.

To the unpracticed eye, of course, the absence of reading may be almost indistinguishable at times from non-reading; I will concede that nothing more closely resembles one person not reading than a second person not reading either. But if we watch as these two people are confronted with a book, the difference in their behavior and its underlying motivation will be readily apparent.

In the first case, the person not reading is not interested in the book, but *book* is understood here both as content and location. The book's relationship to others is as much a matter of indifference to him as its subject, and he is not in the least concerned that in taking an interest in one book, he might seem to disdain the rest.

In the second case, the person not reading abstains, like Musil's librarian, in order to grasp the essence of the book, which is how it fits into the library as a whole. In so doing, he is hardly uninterested in the book—to the contrary. It is because he understands the link between content and location that he chooses not to read, with a wisdom superior to that of many readers, and perhaps, on reflection, with greater respect for the book itself.

Books You Have Skimmed

(in which we see, along with Valéry, that
it is enough to have skimmed a book
to be able to write an article about it, and
that with certain books it might even
be inappropriate to do otherwise)

THE IDEA OF OVERALL PERSPECTIVE has implications for
more than just situating a book within the collective library;
it is equally relevant to the task of situating each passage
within a book. The cultivated reader will find that the orientation skills he has developed with regard to the library function just as well within a single volume. Being culturally
literate means being able to get your bearings quickly in a
book, which does not require reading the book in its
entirety—quite the opposite, in fact. One might even argue
that the greater your abilities in this area, the less will it be
necessary to read any book in particular.

The attitude of the librarian in *The Man Without Qualities*
represents an extreme position held by few people, even

among those opposed to reading, for in the end it is quite difficult to choose never to read at all. More common is the case of the reader who does not shun books entirely, but is content to skim them. The behavior of the heroic librarian is somewhat ambiguous in this regard, moreover, since although he is careful not to open any books, he is still interested in their titles and tables of contents, and so develops an impression of the work whether he means to or not.

Skimming books without actually reading them does not in any way prevent you from commenting on them. It's even possible that this is the most efficient way to absorb books, respecting their inherent depth and richness without getting lost in the details. Such, in any case, was the opinion—and the declared practice—of that master of non-reading Paul Valéry.

~

In the gallery of writers who have warned of the risks of reading, Valéry occupies a significant place, having devoted a portion of his work to denouncing this dangerous activity. Monsieur Teste, the Valéryan hero par excellence, lives in an apartment empty of books. Quite plausibly he is modeled in this regard (as in many others) on the writer, who makes no secret of the fact that he does not read much: "Initially, I took an aversion to reading and even divided up among my friends the books I liked best. I was obliged to buy several of them back later on, after the acute phase. But I am not much of a reader, since what I look for in a work is what will enable or impede an aspect of my own activity."[1]

This mistrust of books was directed first and foremost against biography. Valéry achieved a certain fame in the world of literary criticism by calling into question the common practice of linking a work closely to its author. It was conventional in nineteenth-century criticism to maintain that knowledge of the author enhanced that of the work, and thus to amass as much information about him as possible.

Breaking with that critical tradition, Valéry posited that despite appearances, an author is in no position to explain his own work. The work is the product of a creative process that occurs in the writer but transcends him, and it is unfair to reduce the work to that act of creation. To understand a text, therefore, there is little point in gathering information about the author, since in the final analysis he serves it only as a temporary shelter.

Valéry was far from the only writer of his era to advocate a separation between the work and its author. In his post-humously published book *Against Sainte-Beuve*,[2] Proust advanced the theory that a literary work is the product of a different self from the person we know; in *A la recherche de temps perdu*,[3] he illustrated this theory through the character of Bergotte. But Valéry was not satisfied with eliminating the author from the domain of literary criticism; pressing his advantage, he sought to drive him out of the text as well.

---

1. Paul Valéry, *Oeuvres I* (Paris: Gallimard Pléiade, 1957), p. 1479, SB+.
2. HB+.
3. SB and HB++.

~

Though Valéry did not read much, this did not prevent him from having precise opinions on the authors about whom he knew so little, and discussing these authors at length.

Like most people who talk about Proust, Valéry had never read him. But unlike most, he was unfazed by this fact, and with serene cynicism he began his tribute to Proust in the January 1923 issue of the *Nouvelle Revue Française*, shortly after the writer's death, with these words:

> Although I have scarcely read a single volume of Marcel Proust's great work, and although the very art of the novelist is an art that I find inconceivable, I am nevertheless well aware, from the little of the *Recherche du temps perdu* that I have found time to read, what an exceptionally heavy loss literature has just suffered; and not only literature but still more that secret society composed of those who in every age give the age its real value.[4]

His shamelessness shows no signs of abating as the introduction continues, for in justifying his lack of knowledge of the author he is discussing, he is reduced to taking refuge in the favorable (and, more important, convergent) assessments of André Gide and Léon Daudet:

---

4. Paul Valéry, *Masters and Friends*, translated by Martin Turnell (Princeton: Princeton University Press, 1968), p. 295.

In any case, even if I had never read a line of Proust's vast work, the mere fact that two people with minds as different as Gide and Léon Daudet were agreed about its importance would have been sufficient to allay any doubts; such unexpected agreement could only occur in the case of a virtual certainty. We can be easy in our minds; the sun must be shining if they both proclaim the fact at the same time.[5]

Other people's views are thus an essential prerequisite to forming an opinion of your own. In fact, you might even be able to rely on them entirely, to the point—one assumes that such was the case for Valéry—that it might be unnecessary to read a single line of the text. The trouble with this blind reliance on other readers is, as Valéry acknowledges, that it is then hard to comment on the text with any specificity:

Others will speak with authority and penetration of the power and subtlety of Proust's work. Still others will tell us what manner of man it was who conceived the work and brought it to a glorious conclusion; I myself merely caught a glimpse of him many years ago. I can therefore only put forward a view without weight and barely worth recording. Let it be no more than a tribute, a fading flower on a tomb that will endure.[6]

---

5. Ibid.
6. Ibid.

If we can credit Valéry for his sincerity and manage to look past his cynicism, we are likely to concede that the several pages on Proust that follow are not without truth, demonstrating something we will have occasion to observe again and again: it is not at all necessary to be familiar with what you're talking about in order to talk about it accurately.

After the introduction, Valéry's article is divided into two sections. The first deals with the novel in general, and here one can sense that the author is in no rush to offer any specific observations. We thus learn that the novel is intent on "conveying to us one or several imaginary 'lives,' which it institutes as characters, whose time and place are determined, whose adventures are formulated"—a characteristic that distinguishes it from poetry and allows it to be summarized and translated without great loss. These remarks, true enough in the case of many novels, are in fact hardly applicable to Proust, whose work is hard to summarize. But Valéry shows greater inspiration in the second part of his text.

This section is devoted to Proust, whom it is difficult to avoid mentioning entirely. Valéry brings him up in the context of a broader trend in writing ("Proust turned such a loose and simple structure to the most extraordinary account"), but then teases out the author's specificity, based on the manifestly Proustian notion that his work explores the "overabundance of echoes that the least image awakened in the author's very substance."[7] There are two advantages to concentrating on the Proustian habit of playing on an image's

7. Ibid., p. 298.

infinite associations. First of all, you don't need to have read Proust to be aware of it; you need merely open his work to any page to observe this technique in action. Second, it is a strategic choice in that it justifies Valéry's own approach, since Proust's habit of drawing associations from the smallest detail might seem to encourage a critic to do likewise with Proust's work, as opposed to actually reading it.

Shrewdly, Valéry explains that the value of Proust's work lies in its remarkable ability to be opened at random to any page:

> The interest of his work lies in each fragment. We can open the book wherever we choose; its vitality does not depend on what went before, on a sort of *acquired illusion*; it depends on what might be called the *active properties* of the very tissue of the text.[8]

Valéry's stroke of genius lies in showing that his method of non-reading is actually necessitated by the author, and that abstaining from reading Proust's work is the greatest compliment he can give him. Thus, as he concludes his article (with a tribute to "difficult authors" who will soon be understood by no one), he barely conceals that, having accomplished his critical task, he has no more intention of reading Proust than ever.

~

If his tribute to Proust allowed Valéry to illustrate his conception of reading, it was one of Proust's major contemporaries,

---

8. Ibid. Valéry's emphasis.

Anatole France, who gave Valéry the pretext to show his full powers as a critic depended neither on author nor text.

In 1925, the Académie Française invited Valéry to fill the chair left vacant by Anatole France, and in the way of things, Valéry was therefore forced to eulogize him. Valéry diligently avoided following the responsibility he outlined for himself in the opening of his address:

> The dead have but one last resort: the living. Our thoughts are their only access to the light of day. They who have taught us so much, who seem to have bowed out for our sake and forfeited to us their advantages, ought by all rights to be reverently summoned to our memories and invited to drink a draught of life through our words.[9]

If he had hoped to live on in the thoughts of others, Anatole France would have done well to find some other eulogizer than Valéry, who employs all of his ingenuity in the oration so as not to pay tribute to France. His speech is an endless series of perfidious jabs at his predecessor, barely disguised as compliments:

> The public could not thank my illustrious predecessor enough for giving them water in the desert. By contrast with the highly complex and explosive styles being developed on all sides, the measured cadences of his writing proved mildly and agreeably surprising. It was as though

---

9. Paul Valéry, *Occasions*, translated by Roger Shattuck and Frederick Brown (Princeton: Princeton University Press, 1970), p. 4.

fluency, clarity, and simplicity, the patron goddesses of the average man, had returned to earth. Those who prefer the sort of writing that gives them pleasure without requiring much thought took an immediate fancy to his work, whose seductive charm lay in its totally unaffected appearance, whose limpidity sometimes allowed a deeper thought, but nothing to mystify: his work remains, however, unfailingly readable, if not wholly reassuring. He perfected the art of brushing lightly over the most serious ideas and problems. Nothing in his book gives the least difficulty unless it be the wonder itself of encountering none.[10]

It is hard to imagine a denser assemblage of injurious implications in so few lines. France's work is successively characterized as "gentle," "agreeable," "refreshing," "measured," and "simple," terms that in literary criticism do not generally pass for compliments. What is more, and this is the kicker, France's work is apt to please everyone. It can be savored mindlessly, since ideas are only "brushed over"—an evaluation to which Valéry adds:

> What could be more precious than the delectable illusion, created by such clarity, that we are enriching ourselves with ease, deriving pleasure without pain, comprehending without giving our attention, enjoying a free show?

---

10. Ibid., pp. 12–13.

Blessed are those writers who relieve us of the burden of thought, and who dexterously weave a luminous
veil over the complexity of things.[11]

If Valéry's tribute to France is a protracted exercise in nas-
tiness, its most brutal achievement may be its vagueness; it
is as though Valéry wished to convey that to read Anatole
France's work at all would be a betrayal of his low opinion.
Not only are no titles mentioned, but his speech is unblem-
ished by even a single allusion to any of France's works.

Worse yet, Valéry is careful never to mention the name of
the individual whose chair he is preparing to occupy, desig-
nating him through circumlocution or allusively by way of a
play on his name: "He himself could have been possible and
even conceivable only in France, whose name he adopted as
his own."[12]

Valéry's refusal to give the impression that he has read
Anatole France may also be a function of the greatest fault he
imputes to his fellow author: that he read too much. He char-
acterizes France as an "infinite reader"—which, coming from
Valéry, sounds like an insult—who, in opposition to his suc-
cessor in the Académie, was inclined to lose himself among
books:

I must say, gentlemen, that the mere thought of all those
immense stacks of printed pages mounting throughout
the world is enough to shake the stoutest heart. There is

11. Ibid., p. 13.
12. Ibid., p. 20.

nothing more likely to confuse and unbalance the mind than scanning the gilt-lined walls of a huge library, no sight could be more painful to the mind than those shoals of volumes, those parapets of intellectual produce that rise along the quais, the millions of tomes and pamphlets foundered on the bank of the Seine like waste, abandoned there by the stream of time thus purging itself of our thoughts.[13]

This excessive reading, he implies, stripped France of originality. Indeed, in Valéry's eyes, such is the principal risk of reading to the writer—that of subordinating him to others:

Your learned and subtle colleague, gentlemen, did not feel this unease in the face of great numbers. He had a stronger head. Unlike those who are subject to statistical vertigo and revulsion, he did not need to take the precaution of reading very little. Far from being oppressed, he was stimulated by all this wealth, freely drawing upon it to direct and sustain his own art, with happy results.

More than one critic has taken him to task rather harshly, and naïvely, for being so knowledgeable and for not being unaware of what he knew. What was he supposed to do? What did he do that had not always been done? Nothing is newer than the standard of absolute newness imposed as an obligation on writers.[14]

---

13. Ibid., p. 23.
14. Ibid., p. 24.

Key to this passage is the condition, so antithetical to France's way of proceeding, of "being unaware of what you know." With cultural literacy comes the inherent threat of vanishing in other people's books, a threat it is vital to escape if we are to create any work of our own. France, who never managed to blaze a path of his own, perfectly epitomizes the damage that stands to be done by reading; small wonder, then, that Valéry is careful not only never to quote or evoke his work, but never even to say his name, as though this alone might curse Valéry with a similar diminution of self.

∼

The problem with these "tributes" to Proust and Anatole France is that in effect they cast doubt on all of Valéry's other writing about writers, forcing us to question whether he has read their work or barely skimmed it. Once Valéry acknowledges that he hardly reads at all and yet doesn't hesitate to offer his opinion, even his most innocuous critical declarations become suspect.

The tribute he offers to the third great name of French letters in the first half of the century, Henri Bergson, is hardly calculated to set our minds at ease. This text, entitled "A Discourse on Bergson," is drawn from a lecture delivered at the Académie Française in January 1941, on the occasion of the philosopher's death. It begins, rather traditionally, with an evocation of Bergson's death and funeral, before launching into a list of his qualities, described in the most wooden terms imaginable:

He was the pride of our Society. Whether or not we
were attracted by his metaphysics, whether or not we
had followed him in the profound researches to which
he devoted the whole of his life, and in the truly creative
evolution of his thought, which became steadily bolder
and more independent, we possessed in him the most
authentic example of the highest intellectual virtues.[15]

One would expect, after such an introduction, that these
compliments might receive a bit of justification, and—why
not?—that Valéry might specify his positions in relation to
those of Bergson. But this illusion is swift to evaporate, for the
formula that begins the following paragraph is one customarily
reserved for commentaries on texts that have not been read:

I do not propose to discuss his philosophy. This is not
the moment to undertake an examination which would
need to be searching and which could only be so if it
were done in the light of brighter days and by means of
the full and unfettered exercise of thought.[16]

We may well fear, in the case of Valéry, that his refusal to
examine Bergson's philosophy is not just figurative but literal.
The remainder of the text is far from reassuring:

The very ancient and for that reason very difficult
problems with which M. Bergson dealt, those of time,

15. *Masters and Friends,* p. 303.
16. Ibid.

memory, and above all the evolution of life, were through him given a new beginning, and the position of philosophy as it appeared in France fifty years ago has undergone a remarkable change.[17]

Saying that Bergson worked on time and memory—what philosopher has not?—can hardly be passed off as a description, even a succinct one, of his work in its originality. With the exception of a few lines on the opposition between Bergson and Kant, the rest of the text is so vague that, although it describes Bergson perfectly well, it could equally apply to many other philosophers:

A very lofty, very pure and superior exemplar of the thinking man, and perhaps one of the last men who will have devoted himself exclusively, profoundly, and nobly to thinking, in a period when the world thinks and meditates less and less, when, with each day that passes, civilization is further reduced to the memories and vestiges we keep of its multifarious riches and its free and abundant intellectual production, while poverty, suffering, and restrictions of every kind discourage and depress all intellectual enterprise, Bergson seems already to belong to a past age and his name to be the last great name in the history of the European mind.[18]

---

17. Ibid.
18. Ibid., p. 306.

As we see, Valéry is unable to resist ending on a malevolent note, the warmhearted phrase "the last great name in the history of the European mind" mitigating only with difficulty the harshness of the one preceding it, which cordially consigns Bergson to "a past age." Reading these words, in full recognition of Valéry's passion for books, one may well worry that he chose to emphasize the philosopher's outmoded position within the history of ideas in order to dispense with opening any of his works.

∾

This practice of criticism without reference to author or text is in no way absurd. In Valéry's case, it is based on a reasoned conception of literature, one of whose principal ideas is that not only is the author useless, but the work itself is really a bit gratuitous as well.

This embarrassment around the work may be related first of all to Valéry's whole notion of literature, what he calls, following Aristotle and others, a *poetics*. More than anything, he is concerned with developing the general laws of literature. It follows that the position of each text becomes ambiguous: it can serve as an example within the elaboration of that poetics, to be sure, but at the same time it is also just what may be put aside to achieve a view of the whole.

We may thus follow William Marx in noting that what interests Valéry is less a specific work than its "idea":

Just as academic criticism sought to accumulate the greatest number of documents possible and accorded to extra-literary sources (correspondences, private papers, etc.) preeminent importance in its efforts, criticism in the mode of Valéry sought to limit its object to the maximum extent possible, to the point where it no longer retained in its field of observation anything but the work itself, or even less than the work: the simple idea of the work.[19]

According to this model, we have all a greater likelihood of grasping this idea, this "less than the work," if we do not get too close to it, where we risk getting lost in its details. To take this theory to its extreme, what is interesting about a text—which is not the work itself, but the qualities it shares with others—might be best perceived by a critic who closes his eyes in the presence of the work and thinks, instead, about what it may be. On these grounds, any overly attentive reading, if not indeed all reading, is an obstacle to our deepest understanding of a book.

With this poetics of distance, Valéry offers rational grounds for one of our most common ways of interacting with books: skimming. When we have a book in our hands, it is rare that we read it from cover to cover, assuming such a feat is possible at all. Most of the time, we do with books what Valéry recommends doing with Proust: we skim them.

The notion of skimming or flipping through books can be understood in at least two different senses. In the first case, the skimming is linear. The reader begins the text at the beginning,

---

19. William Marx, *Naissance de la critique moderne* (Artois: Presses Université, 2002), p. 25, SB+.

then starts skipping lines or pages as, successfully or not, he makes his way toward the end. In the second case, the skimming is circuitous: rather than read in an orderly fashion, the reader takes a stroll through the work, sometimes beginning at the end. This second method implies no more ill will on the part of the reader than does the first. It simply constitutes one of our habitual ways of relating to books.

But the fertility of this mode of discovery markedly unsettles the difference between reading and non-reading, or even the idea of reading at all. In which category do we place the behavior of those who have spent a certain amount of time on a book—hours, even—without reading it completely? Should they be inclined to discuss it, is it fair to say of them that they are talking about a book they haven't read? The same question may be raised with regard to those who, like Musil's librarian, remain in the margins of the book. Who, we may wonder, is the better reader—the person who reads a work in depth without being able to situate it, or the person who enters no book in depth, but circulates through them all?

As we see, it is difficult—and things will only get worse—to delimit just what non-reading is, or indeed reading, for that matter. It appears that most often, at least for the books that are central to our particular culture, our behavior inhabits some intermediate territory, to the point that it becomes difficult to judge whether we have read them or not.

≈

Just as Musil does, Valéry prompts us to think in terms of a collective library rather than a solitary book. For a true reader, one who cares about being able to reflect on literature, it is not any specific book that counts, but the totality of all books. Paying exclusive attention to an individual volume causes us to risk losing sight of that totality, as well as the qualities in each book that figure in the larger scheme.

But Valéry goes further, inviting us to adapt that same attitude to each book, maintaining a broad perspective over it that works in tandem with a broad view of books as a group. In our quest for this perspective, we must guard against getting lost in any individual passage, for it is only by maintaining a reasonable distance from the book that we may be able to appreciate its true meaning.

III

Books You Have Heard Of

(in which Umberto Eco shows that it is wholly
unnecessary to have held a book in your hand to
be able to speak about it in detail, as long as you
listen to and read what others say about it)

THE LOGICAL IMPLICATION of this theory—that cultural literacy involves the dual capacity to situate books in the collective library and to situate yourself within each book—is that it is ultimately unnecessary to have handled a book to have a sense of it and to express your thoughts on the subject. The act of reading is disassociated from the material book; the important thing is the encounter, which might just as easily involve an immaterial object.

Besides actually reading a book, there is, after all, another way to develop quite a clear sense of its contents: we can read or listen to what others write or say about it. This tactic (which, as you may recall, Valéry freely employed in the case of Proust) can save you a lot of time. It can also be necessary when a book is lost or has disappeared, or, as we shall see, when the quest for it imperils the life of the person wishing to read it.

This is, in fact, the extent to which we have access to most books, most of the time. Many of the books we are led to talk about, and which have, in certain cases, played important roles in our lives, have never actually passed through our hands (although we may sometimes be convinced of the contrary). But the way other people talk to us or to each other about these books, in their texts or conversations, allows us to forge an idea of their contents, and even to formulate a reasonable opinion of them.

∼

In *The Name of the Rose*,[1] a novel set in the Middle Ages, Umberto Eco describes how a monk named William of Baskerville, accompanied by a young man named Adso—who writes the story many years later, when he himself is an old man—arrives to conduct an investigation in an abbey in northern Italy, where a suspicious death has occurred.

At the center of the abbey an immense library has been built in the form of a labyrinth; its holdings are the largest in all of Christendom. This library occupies a major place within the religious community and thus within the novel—both as a place of study and reflection, and as at the heart of a whole system of interdictions governing the right to read, since books are delivered to the monks only after authorization.

In his search for the truth about the murders, Baskerville finds himself in competition with the Inquisition and its

---

1. SB and HB++.

formidable representative, Bernard Gui, who is convinced that the crimes are the work of heretics—specifically, the adepts of Dolcino, the founder of a sect hostile to the papacy. Through torture, Gui wrests from several monks confessions that support his views. Baskerville, meanwhile, remains unconvinced of the accuracy of his reasoning.

Indeed, Baskerville has arrived at a different conclusion. He believes that the deaths have no direct relation to heresy, and that the monks have been killed for having attempted to read a mysterious book guarded jealously within the library. He gradually formulates an idea of the contents of the book and the reasons why its guardian has resorted to murder. His violent confrontation with the murderer, in the last pages of the novel, sets off a massive fire in the library, which the monks save from destruction only at great cost.

~

In this final scene, then, the investigator comes face-to-face with the murderer. This turns out to be Jorge, one of the oldest monks in the abbey, who has lost his sight. Jorge congratulates Baskerville for having solved the mystery and, apparently admitting his defeat, hands him the book that has led to so many deaths. A heterogeneous volume, the book includes an Arabic text, a Syrian text, an interpretation of the *Coena Cypriani*[2]—a parody of the Bible—and a fourth text in Greek, the one responsible for the murders.

---

2. UB–.

This book, hidden among the others, is the lost second volume of Aristotle's celebrated *Poetics*.[3] In this second volume, which at the time was not yet listed in bibliographies, the Greek philosopher is known to have continued his reflections on literature, this time exploring the theme of laughter.

Jorge responds strangely to Baskerville's accusations. Rather than preventing the investigator from consulting the book, he instead challenges him to read it. Baskerville agrees, but first takes the precaution of arming himself with a pair of gloves. Thus equipped, he opens the book to discover the first lines of a text that he believes to have claimed several victims:

> In the first book we dealt with tragedy and saw how, by arousing pity and fear, it produces catharsis, the purification of those feelings. As we promised, we will now deal with comedy (as well as with satire and mime) and see how, in inspiring the pleasure of the ridiculous, it arrives at the purification of that passion. That such passion is most worthy of consideration we have already said in the book on the soul, inasmuch as—alone among the animals—man is capable of laughter. We will then define the types of actions of which comedy is the mimesis, then we will examine the means by which comedy excites laughter, and these means are actions and speech. We will show how the ridiculousness of actions is born from the likening of the best to the worst and vice versa [. . .] We will then show how the

---

3. HB+.

ridiculousness of speech is born from the misunder-
standings of similar words for different things and different words for similar things, etc.[4]

It would seem to be confirmed, especially given the evocation of other titles by Aristotle, that this mysterious work is
indeed the second volume of the *Poetics*. After reading the
first page and translating it into Latin, Baskerville attempts to
leaf through the following pages. But he encounters a material difficulty, since the deteriorated pages are stuck to each
other and he cannot separate them while wearing gloves.
Jorge exhorts him to keep leafing through the book, but
Baskerville firmly refuses to do so.

He has understood that to keep turning the pages, he would
have to take off his gloves and moisten his fingertips, and that
in so doing he would poison himself, just as the other monks
who had come too close to the truth. Jorge has decided to dis-
patch troublesome researchers by applying poison to the upper
part of the book, where the reader places his fingers. It is an
exemplary murder, in which the victim poisons himself to the
very extent that he violates Jorge's ban and continues to read.

∼

But why systematically execute those who are interested in the
second volume of Aristotle's *Poetics*? When William questions
him, Jorge confirms what the monk-detective has intuited.

4. Umberto Eco, *The Name of the Rose*, translated by William Weaver (New
York: Harcourt, 1983), p. 468.

The murders were committed to prevent the monks from gaining knowledge of the contents of this book. Rather than condemning laughter, the book dignifies it as an object worthy of study—and to Jorge, laughter is antithetical to faith. By reserving the right to turn anything into an object of derision, it opens the path to doubt, which is the enemy of revealed truth:

> "But what frightened you in this discussion of laughter? You cannot eliminate laughter by eliminating the book."
>
> "No, to be sure. But laughter is weakness, corruption, the foolishness of our flesh. It is the peasant's entertainment, the drunkard's license; even the church in her wisdom has granted the moment of feast, carnival, fair, this diurnal pollution that releases humors and distracts from other desires and other ambitions . . . Still, laughter remains base, a defense for the simple, a mystery desecrated for the plebeians [. . .] But here, here"—now Jorge struck the table with his finger, near the book William was holding open—"here the function of laughter is reversed, it is elevated to art, the doors of the learned of the world are opened to it, it becomes the object of philosophy and of perfect theology."[5]

Laughter is thus a threat to faith in that it serves as a vehicle for various forms of doubt. This threat is all the more significant in that the book's author is Aristotle, whose influence was considerable in the Middle Ages:

---

5. Ibid., p. 473.

"There are many other books that speak of comedy, many others that praise laughter. Why did this one fill you with such fear?"

"Because it was by the Philosopher. Every book by that man has destroyed a part of the learning that Christianity had accumulated over the centuries. The fathers had said everything that needed to be known about the power of the Word, but then Boethius had only to gloss the Philosopher and the divine mystery of the Word was transformed into a human parody of categories and syllogism. The book of Genesis says what has to be known about the composition of the cosmos, but it sufficed to rediscover the *Physics* of the Philosopher to have the universe reconceived in terms of dull and slimy matter [. . .] Every word of the Philosopher, by whom now even saints and prophets swear, has overturned the image of the world. But he has not succeeded in overturning the image of God. If this book were to become . . . had become an object for interpretation, we would have crossed the last boundary."[6]

So it is not laughter alone, but the stamp of Aristotle's approval that, for Jorge, constitutes a danger for religion and justifies the murders. With the backing of a philosopher of such stature, the theory that laughter is beneficent—or simply not harmful—risks being broadly disseminated, which might

6. Ibid.

subliminally undermine Christian doctrine. From Jorge's point of view, keeping the book out of the hands of the monks is a pious deed well worth a few victims. Their lives are the price paid for rescuing true faith and protecting it from interrogation.

∾

How did Baskerville arrive at the truth? He has not held the book in his hands until this last scene—in which, moreover, he takes care not to have any direct physical contact with it— and much less has he read it. But he has, all the same, formed a relatively exact sense of it, so much so that he is able to describe its contents to Jorge:

> "Gradually, this second book took shape in my mind as it had to be. I could tell you almost all of it, without reading the pages that were meant to poison me. Comedy is born from the komai—that is, from the peasant villages—as a joyous ceremony after a meal or a feast. Comedy does not tell of famous and powerful men, but of base and ridiculous creatures, though not wicked; it does not end with the death of the protagonists. It achieves the effect of the ridiculous by showing the defects and vices of ordinary men. Here Aristotle sees the tendency to laughter as a force for good, which can also have an instructive value: through witty riddles and unexpected metaphors, though it tells us things differently from the way they are, as if it were lying, it actually obliges us to examine them more closely, and it makes

us say: Ah, this is just how things are, and I didn't know
it [. . .] Is that it?"[7]

It is possible, then, to speak with relative precision ("I
could tell you almost all of it") about a book one has never
held in one's hands, a point of no small interest in a case
where touching the book would be fatal. We derive this ability from the fact that every book is governed by a certain
logic, that logic so interesting to Valéry that he embraced it to
the exclusion of all else. Aristotle's book functions first of all
as an extension of his *Poetics*, which Baskerville knows well.
Having intuited the subject of the second book, and knowing
the trajectory of the first one, Baskerville is able to predict
the forbidden book's general outlines.

The book obeys a second kind of logic, that of its internal
development, which Baskerville is also able to reconstitute
based on Aristotle's other books. A book's means of progres-
sion is never completely idiosyncratic. All works by the same
author present more or less perceptible similarities of structure, and beyond their manifest differences, they secretly share
a common way of ordering reality.

But a third and equally important element, this one not
intrinsic to the work, but external, makes it possible to gain
a sense of the contents of Aristotle's book—namely, the reactions that it has provoked. A book is not limited to itself,
but from the moment of dissemination also encompasses the
exchanges it inspires. To observe these exchanges, then, is

---

7. Ibid., p. 471.

tantamount to gaining access to the book, if not actually to reading it.

It is through just such exchanges that Baskerville has come to know the contents of Aristotle's book. When Jorge, in astonishment and admiration ("Not bad," he says[8]), asks him how he reconstituted a book he has never held in his hands, Baskerville explains that his inspiration was the research conducted by Venantius, the murdered monk who preceded him in his quest and left certain clues behind:

> "[I was helped by several notes left by Venantius.] At first I didn't understand their significance. But there were references to a shameless stone that rolls over the plain, and to cicadas that will sing from the ground, to venerable fig trees. I had already read something of the sort: I verified it during these past few days. These are examples that Aristotle used in the first book of the *Poetics*, and in the *Rhetoric*.[9] Then I remembered that Isidore of Seville defines comedy as something that tells of stupra virginum et amores meretricum . . ."[10]

Through these written exchanges about the book (Venantius's notes), but also through spoken exchanges (comments by those who approached the mysterious book, sometimes without realizing it), and reactions to it (beginning, of course,

---

8. Ibid.
9. UB+.
10. Eco, op. cit., p. 471.

with the murders), Baskerville has gained an increasingly clear sense of the volume before it enters his possession, enough, even, to re-create it in its absence. However original and scandalous it might be, this book, like any other, is not an isolated object but part and parcel of the collective library.

This book, moreover, figures in a collective library whose foundations it stands to undermine, and it is for precisely this reason that Jorge resorts to murder. The book is a threat to the abbey's library, first of all, since it risks attracting the monks to that site of discovery and perdition that is culture. But from Jorge's perspective, Aristotle's second volume also jeopardizes another library without walls—the collective library of man. Our reading of the other books in that library, starting with the Bible, would forever be modified by Aristotle's work. Within the interminable chain that links all books together, a single book has the capacity to displace every other one.

∼

The celebrated plot of *The Name of the Rose* obscures two important and related elements in Eco's novel that bear on our subject. First of all, it is not through implacable logic (as the name of the investigator and his precise conclusion about the contents of Aristotle's book might lead one to think) but, in fact, through a series of false deductions that Baskerville arrives at the truth.

If the final conversation with Jorge allows Baskerville to unmask the alleged murderer, it also shows him the extent to which he has gone astray in his reasoning. Based on his analysis of the first deaths, Baskerville has concluded that the

murderer was literally following the prophecies of the Apoc-
alypse, and that the nature of the crimes was in keeping with
the text on the seven trumpets.[11]

In reality, as is revealed only after the fact, his search for the
truth has been further confounded by the fact that Jorge, spy-
ing on Baskerville and seeing him home in on his Apocalypse-
based interpretation of the murders, decided to lure him
further into error by planting a number of false clues designed
to encourage him in his thesis. To make matters even more
dizzying, in deceiving Baskerville the murderer ended up deceiving himself, becoming persuaded that the deaths were indeed occurring according to a providential plan.[12] Thus
Baskerville is led to observe that he has reached the truth, but
only thanks to the random accumulation of his errors:

> I conceived a false pattern to interpret the moves of the
> guilty man, and the guilty man fell in with it. And it was
> this same false pattern that put me on your trail.[13]

Baskerville's many false deductions raise another problem,
which the book does not confront directly but only suggests:
namely, it invites us to wonder whether his ultimate solution is
correct after all. If we admit that Baskerville has succeeded in
identifying the culprit and the book not through correct rea-

---

11. Certain deaths are not even attributable to Jorge. One of the monks committed suicide; another was murdered by a different monk.
12. "Alinardo had told me about his idea, and then I heard from someone that
you too had found it persuasive . . . I became convinced that a divine plan was
directing these deaths, for which I was not responsible." Eco, op. cit., p. 470.
13. Ibid.

soning but through a series of erroneous deductions, then there
is no guarantee that his conclusions are accurate. Given an investigator who never ceases to get things wrong, we may be for-
given for not accepting his final conclusions at face value.[14]

.We cannot exclude the possibility of a twofold error about
both the book and the murderer, then, nor can we reject the
notion that Baskerville may have gotten things right in one
case and wrong in the other. That Jorge is the murderer remains to be proven; meanwhile, he may have every reason to
encourage Baskerville in the illusion that the mysterious book
is indeed the second volume of Aristotle's *Poetics*, particularly
if he is intent on protecting an even more formidable book.
The ironic attitude Jorge maintains until the end, without ever
truly authenticating Baskerville's solution, casts a shadow of
doubt over a conclusion that, in the wake of so many accumulated errors, seems at the very least impossible to verify.

≈

Eco's novel illustrates that the books we talk about are only
glancingly related to "real" books—indeed, what else would
we expect?—and are often no more than *screen books*.[15] Or, if
you prefer, what we talk about is not the books themselves,
but substitute objects we create for the occasion.

---

14. See my book *Who Killed Roger Ackroyd?* (New York: New Press, 2000), FB+.
15. Freud uses the term *screen memory* to designate false or insignificant childhood memories whose function is to conceal others less acceptable to the conscious mind. See "Screen Memories," in Sigmund Freud, *The Standard Edition
of the Complete Psychological Works*, vol. 3, translated by James Strachey (London:
Hogarth Press, 1978), p. 307, SB++.

On a purely material level, Aristotle's book is largely a virtual object, since neither Jorge nor Baskerville has access to it. Jorge lost his vision many years before the story begins, and so his notion of the book is based solely on memory, which is further distorted by his madness. As for Baskerville, he can do no more than rapidly skim the book and is forced to rely primarily on his reconstruction of it, the uncertainty of which has already been demonstrated. Without question, then, the two men are speaking about two different books, each having constructed an imaginary object based on his own personal agenda.

The impossibility of accessing the text only serves to highlight its projective nature, as the book becomes the receptacle of both characters' fantasies. To Jorge, Aristotle's book is a locus for his anxieties about threats to the Church, while for Baskerville it provides support for his relativistic reflections on faith. Their fantasies are all the less likely to overlap, other than through shared illusion, in that neither of the two men has, properly speaking, the text in hand.

To convince yourself that any book we may talk about is a screen book, a substitute element in the endless chain of all books, perform the simple experiment of comparing your memory of a book cherished in childhood with the "real" book. The invariable differences demonstrate the extent to which our memory of books, most particularly those that matter to the point where they become part of us, is endlessly reorganized by the unconscious stakes of our present circumstances.

The screen book consists in large part of what the reader knows or believes he knows about the book, and thus to the comments exchanged about it. To a significant extent, our discourse about books focuses on the discourse of other people about those books, and so forth ad infinitum. The abbey's library stands as a luminous symbol of such discourse about discourse, in which the book itself disappears in a fog of language, since libraries are the site par excellence of infinite commentary.

At the core of such discourse is the one we address to ourselves, for our own words about books separate and protect us from them as much as the commentary of others. As soon as we begin to read, and perhaps even before that, we begin talking to ourselves and then to others about books. We will resort thereafter to these comments and opinions, while actual books, now rendered hypothetical, recede forever into the distance.

≈

For Eco even more than Valéry, it seems, the book is an undefined object that we can discuss only in imprecise terms, an object forever buffeted by our fantasies and illusions. The second volume of Aristotle's *Poetics*, impossible to find even in a library of infinite capacity, is no different from most other books we discuss in our lives. They are all reconstructions of originals that lie so deeply buried beneath our words and the words of others that, even were we prepared to risk our lives, we stand little chance of ever finding them within reach.

Books You Have Forgotten

(in which, along with Montaigne, we raise
the question of whether a book you have
read and completely forgotten, and which
you have even forgotten you have read,
is still a book you have read)

AS WE HAVE NOW SEEN, there is not much between a book that has been "read"—if that category still has a meaning—and one that has been skimmed. But Valéry has even better grounds than this for merely flipping through the works he discusses, and Baskerville, likewise, for commenting on books without opening them, which is that the most serious and thorough reading quickly metamorphoses after the fact into summary. To appreciate this, we must take into account a dimension of reading neglected by many theorists: that of time. Reading is not just acquainting ourselves with a text or acquiring knowledge; it is also, from its first moments, an inevitable process of forgetting.

Even as I read, I start to forget what I have read, and this process is unavoidable. It extends to the point where it's as though I haven't read the book at all, so that in effect I find myself rejoining the ranks of non-readers, where I should no doubt have remained in the first place. At this point, saying we have read a book becomes essentially a form of metonymy. When it comes to books, we never read more than a portion of greater or lesser length, and that portion is, in the longer or shorter term, condemned to disappear. When we talk about books, then, to ourselves and to others, it would be more accurate to say that we are talking about our approximate recollections of books, rearranged as a function of current circumstances.

∼

No reader is safe from this process of forgetting, not even the most voracious. Such was the case for Montaigne, who is fundamentally associated with ancient culture and libraries and who nevertheless presents himself, with a frankness that anticipates Valéry, as an eminently forgetful reader.

The flaws of memory are, in fact, a persistent theme in the *Essais*,[1] if not the best known. Montaigne complains endlessly about his memory trouble and the unpleasantness it causes him. He tells us, for example, that he is incapable of going to look for a piece of information in his library without forgetting on the way what he is looking for. When speaking, he finds it necessary to maintain a tightly

---

1. SB and HB++.

ordered discourse so as not to lose his train of thought. And he is so unable to remember names that he resolves to refer to his servants according to their jobs or countries of origin.

The problem grows so serious that Montaigne, always on the brink of an identity crisis, occasionally fears that he will forget his own name. He even goes so far as to ponder how he will navigate daily life on the inevitable day that such a misadventure occurs.

This general faultiness of memory plainly affects the books he has read. Toward the beginning of his essay on his reading, Montaigne unhesitatingly acknowledges his difficulty in keeping track of what he has read: "And if I am a man of some reading," he declares, "I am a man of no retentiveness."[2]

Montaigne experiences a progressive and systematic erasure that attacks every component of the book from the author to the text itself, each vanishing one after the other from his memory as quickly as it entered:

> I leaf through books, I do not study them. What I retain of them is something I no longer recognize as anyone else's. It is only the material from which my judgment has profited, and the thoughts and ideas with which it has become imbued; the author, the place, the words, and other circumstances, I immediately forget.[3]

---

2. The *Complete Essays of Montaigne*, translated by Donald Frame (Stanford: Stanford University Press, 1957), p. 296.
3. Ibid., p. 494.

This effacement, in other words, is the flip side of an en-
richment. Having made the text his own, Montaigne rushes
to forget it, as though a book were no more than a temporary
delivery system for some general form of wisdom and, its
mission accomplished, might as well disappear. But the fact
that the implications of forgetting are not altogether negative
does not solve all its associated problems, especially the psychological ones. Nor does it dispel the anguish, intensified by
the daily obligation of speaking to others, of not being able
to fix anything in one's memory.

~

It is true that we all experience mishaps of this sort, and that
all literature ends up providing us only a fragile and temporary kind of knowledge. What seems particular to the case of
Montaigne, however, and indicates the breadth of his problems with memory, is his inability to recall whether he has
read a specific book:

To compensate a little for the treachery and weakness
of my memory, so extreme that it has happened to me
more than once to pick up again, as recent and unknown to me, books which I had read carefully a few
years before and scribbled over with my notes, I have
adopted the habit for some time now of adding at the
end of each book (I mean of those I intend to use only
once) the time I finished reading it and the judgment I
have derived of it as a whole, so that this may represent

to me at least the sense and general idea I had conceived
of the author in reading it.[4]

The memory deficit is revealed as even more acute in this
case, since it is no longer just the book but the experience of
reading that is forgotten. Here, the forgetting erases not just
the contents of the object—whose general shape, at least, can
still be called to mind—but the act of reading itself, as though
the radical nature of the erasure had ended up affecting everything related to the object. We would be justified in such circumstances in wondering whether reading that we cannot
even remember performing still deserves to be called reading.

Curiously, Montaigne displays a relatively precise memory
of certain books he dislikes; he is, for instance, capable of dis-
tinguishing different kinds of texts by Cicero or even the different books of the *Aeneid*.[5] One gets the impression that
these texts in particular—conceivably because they made a
deeper impression than the others—have escaped oblivion.
Here, too, the affective factor proves decisive in the substitution of a screen book for the hypothetical real book.

Montaigne finds a solution to his memory problem
through an ingenious system of notations at the end of each
volume. Once forgetfulness has set in, he can use these notes
to rediscover his opinion of the author and his work at the
time of his original reading. We can assume that another
function of the notes is to assure him that he has indeed read

---

4. Ibid., p. 305.
5. HB++.

the works in which they were inscribed, like blazes on a trail that are intended to show the way during future periods of amnesia.

≈

What follows in this essay about reading is even more astonishing. After explaining the principle behind his notational system, Montaigne unflappably presents the reader with a few excerpts. In doing so, he tells the reader about books that it is hard to say whether he has read, since he has forgotten their contents and must rely on his own notations—writing, for example, "Here is what I put some ten years ago in my Guicciardini (for whatever language my books speak, I speak to them in my own)."[6]

The first author "discussed" is indeed the Renaissance historian Guicciardini, whom Montaigne deems to be a "diligent historiographer," and all the more trustworthy in that he was himself an actor in the events he recounts and seems little inclined to flatter those in power. His second example is Philippe de Commines, for whom Montaigne has unstinting praise, admiring his simplicity of language, narrative purity, and absence of vanity. Third, he evokes the *Memoirs*[7] of du Bellay, an author whose work in public office he admires, but who, he fears, is too much in the service of the king.[8]

---

6. Montaigne, op. cit., p. 305.
7. UB+.
8. Montaigne, op. cit., p. 306.

In reading his notes in order to comment on these texts—
which he may not remember reading, and even if he does,
whose contents he may have forgotten—Montaigne finds himself in a contradictory position. The commentary he is reading
is not exactly his, without its being foreign to him either. He
conveys to his reader the reaction he had to these books on an
earlier occasion, without taking the trouble to verify whether
that reaction coincides with what he might experience today.

For Montaigne, an inveterate practitioner of the art of
quotation, this is an unprecedented situation: instead of citing
other writers, he cites himself. Indeed, at this extreme the distinction between quotation and self-quotation vanishes. Having forgotten what he said about these authors and even that
he said anything at all, Montaigne has become other to himself. He is separated from the earlier incarnation of himself by
the defects of his memory, and his readings of his notes represent so many attempts at reunification.

However surprising we may find Montaigne's reliance on
this system of notes, he is, after all, only drawing out the logical consequence of something known to anyone familiar with
books, whatever the state of his memory. What we preserve of
the books we read—whether we take notes or not, and even if
we sincerely believe we remember them faithfully—is in truth
no more than a few fragments afloat, like so many islands, on
an ocean of oblivion.

≈

The reader of Montaigne has still more surprises ahead of
him. The author goes on to reveal that as forgetful as he may

be of other people's books, to the point where he cannot even recall whether he has read them, he is no more capable of remembering his own:

> It is no great wonder if my book follows the fate of other books, and if my memory lets go of what I write as of what I read, and of what I give as of what I receive.[9]

Incapable of remembering what he has written, Montaigne finds himself confronted with the fear of all those losing their memory: repeating yourself without realizing it, and knowing the anguish of losing mastery over your own writing only to remain unwittingly all too faithful to yourself. His fear is all the more justified in that the *Essais* address not topical subjects, but timeless questions. These may be broached on any occasion, and a writer without memory is thus vulnerable to treating them again without knowing it, and in identical terms:

> Now I am bringing in here nothing newly learned. These are common ideas; having perhaps thought of them a hundred times, I am afraid I have already set them down.[10]

These "repetitions," which Montaigne finds regrettable in an author like Homer, seem to him even more "ruinous" in

---

9. Ibid., p. 494.
10. Ibid., p. 734.

texts like his own, "which attract only superficial and passing attention,"[11] and which he risks rewriting word by word, from one chapter to the next, without even perceiving it.

But fear of repeating himself is not the only embarrassing consequence of forgetting his own books. Another is that Montaigne does not even recognize his own texts when they are quoted in his presence, leaving him to speak about texts he hasn't read even though he has written them.

For Montaigne, therefore, reading is related not only to defective memory, but also, given the contradictions that arise from it, to the anguish of madness. While reading is enriching in the moment it occurs, it is at the same time a source of depersonalization, since, in our inability to stabilize the smallest snippet of text, it leaves us incapable of coinciding with ourselves.

~

With his repeated sense that his self is being eclipsed, Montaigne, more than any of the other authors we have thus far encountered, seems to erase any distinction between reading and non-reading. Indeed, if after being read a book immediately begins to disappear from consciousness, to the point where it becomes impossible to remember whether we have read it, the very notion of reading loses its relevance, since any book, read or unread, will end up the equivalent of any other.

However extreme his case may be, Montaigne's relationship

---

11. Ibid.

with books reveals the true nature of the relationship we all have with them. We do not retain in memory complete books identical to the books remembered by everyone else, but rather fragments surviving from partial readings, frequently fused together and further recast by our private fantasies. In the end we are left with falsified remnants of books, analogous to the screen memories discussed by Freud, whose principal function is to conceal others.

Following Montaigne, we should perhaps use the term *un-reading* rather than reading to characterize the unceasing sweep of our forgetfulness. This process involves both the disappearance and the blurring of references, and transforms books, often reduced to their titles or to a few approximate pages, into dim shadows gliding along the surface of our consciousness.

In every consideration of reading, we should remain mindful that books are linked not only to knowledge, but also to loss of memory and even identity. To read is not only to inform ourselves, but also, and perhaps above all, to forget, and thus to confront our capacity for oblivion.

The *reading subject* that emerges in this essay of Montaigne's is not a unified and self-assured figure but an uncertain one, lost among fragments of texts he can barely identify. For this figure, no longer able to distinguish his own texts from those of others, each encounter with a book becomes terrifying, for it threatens to bring him face-to-face with his own madness.

∾

As agonizing as it may be, Montaigne's experience may nonetheless have the salutary effect of reassuring those to whom cultural literacy seems unattainable. It is vital to keep in mind that the most conscientious readers we might speak to are also, just like Montaigne, involuntary non-readers, and that their forgetfulness extends even to books that in all good faith they believe themselves to have mastered.

To conceive of reading as loss—whether it occurs after we skim a book, in absorbing a book by hearsay, or through the gradual process of forgetting—rather than as gain is a psychological resource essential to anyone seeking effective strategies for surviving awkward literary confrontations. Having defined the different kinds of non-reading, it is to these social situations that we now turn our attention.

Literary Confrontations

Encounters in Society

(in which Graham Greene describes a nightmarish
situation where the hero finds himself facing an
auditorium full of admirers impatiently waiting for
him to speak about books that he hasn't read)

HAVING EXAMINED THE PRINCIPAL KINDS of non-reading,
which, as we have seen, may take more subtle forms than a
simple absence of reading pure and simple, let us now consider several common situations in which the reader (or
rather, the non-reader) finds himself forced to speak about
books he hasn't read. It is my hope that these reflections, inspired by my personal experience, will be of use to the non-
reader in negotiating such situations himself.

The most common literary confrontations are those that
occur in our social lives, and of these the most vexing are
those in which we are expected to express ourselves in front
of a group. On such occasions, the conversation may turn to
a book we have not read. If the book in question is assumed
to be known by all cultivated individuals, or if we make the

error of blurting out that we *have* read it, we may find ourselves forced to try to save face.

This is an unpleasant situation, no doubt, but with a little finesse we may extricate ourselves from it at no great cost—by changing the subject, for example. But it's easy to imagine such a situation turning into a nightmare, in which the person being forced to speak about a book he hasn't read is subjected to the rapt attention of an entire audience eager to know his thoughts. Such circumstances bring to mind what Freud calls the "examination dream," in which the terrified dreamer imagines himself summoned to an exam for which he is not prepared, and which calls back to consciousness a whole series of buried childhood fears.[1]

~

This is indeed what happens to Rollo Martins in *The Third Man*, the Graham Greene novel that inspired Carol Reed's celebrated film. At the beginning of the book, Martins,

---

1. "Everyone who has passed the Matriculation examination at the end of his school studies complains of the obstinacy with which he is pursued by anxiety-dreams of having failed, or of being obliged to take the examination again, etc. In the case of those who have obtained a University degree this typical dream is replaced by another one which represents them as having failed in their University finals; and it is in vain that they object, even while they are still asleep, that for years they have been practicing medicine or working as University lecturers or heads of offices. The ineradicable memories of the punishments that we suffered for our evil deeds in childhood become active within us once more and attach themselves to the two crucial points in our studies—the *dies irae, dies illa* of our stiffest examinations." Sigmund Freud, *The Interpretation of Dreams*, translated by James Strachey (New York: Avon, 1965), p. 308.

the story's protagonist, arrives in postwar Vienna, which has been divided into four sectors respectively controlled by France, England, the United States, and the Soviet Union.

Martins has traveled to Vienna to find his childhood friend Harry Lime, who has asked Martins to come meet him. But when he arrives at Lime's home, he discovers that his friend has just died in an accident, struck down by a car as he left his house. Martins heads to the cemetery where the funeral is being held, and there meets Anna, Lime's mistress, along with a military police officer named Calloway.

In questioning various witnesses in the days that follow, Martins notices a number of contradictions, and he becomes convinced that his friend was the victim not of an accident, but of a murder. Calloway also has doubts about the circumstances of Lime's death, but for other reasons. He knows that Lime was not only the considerate friend Martins remembers, but also an unscrupulous profiteer who took advantage of the postwar period to sell tainted penicillin, whose effects were fatal for those who consumed it.

Meanwhile, Martins has fallen in love with Anna. One day, as he leaves her apartment building, Martins notices a man standing watch in the street, who turns out to be Lime. He is, in fact, still alive and has staged his own disappearance with the help of a few accomplices out of fear of being arrested by the police.

Through one of these accomplices, Martins demands a meeting with Lime. The reunion takes place on the great Ferris wheel of the Prater in Vienna. Lime shows himself to be the sympathetic fellow that Martins has known since childhood, but also offers occasional glimpses of a man without scruples, indifferent to the fate of his victims.

Terrified by what his friend has become, Martins decides
to collaborate with the police and draw Lime into a trap, by
arranging for another meeting. But Lime escapes into the un-
derground sewer system, where he is wounded by the police.
To put an end to his suffering, Martins finishes him off, then
leaves Vienna with Anna at his side.

∼

The central narrative of the detective story is comple-
mented by another more humorous plotline surrounding
Martins's professional activities. He is a writer, though he
doesn't describe himself as such. He owes his modesty to
the fact that he writes not great works of literature, but
westerns, which appear under the pseudonym Buck Dexter
and bear such evocative titles as *The Lonely Horseman of
Santa Fe*.[2]

The pen name Buck Dexter is the basis of a misunderstanding that extends throughout the book. The cultural office of the embassy has, in fact, confused Martins with
another Dexter, whose first name is Benjamin. This Dexter is
a highbrow novelist whose works, bearing such titles as *The
Curved Prow*,[3] occupy the same literary genre as those of
Henry James.

Rather than clear things up, Martins is extremely careful
not to dispel the confusion, for he has arrived in Vienna
without any money, and the mistaken identity is his ticket to

---

2. UB++.
3. UB–.

free lodging in a hotel, which he needs in order to pursue his investigation. But he makes every effort to avoid the representative of the cultural office, Crabbin, for fear of having to fulfill the duties that are Benjamin Dexter's.

Things go awry one evening when Crabbin forces Martins to come deliver a literary lecture to an audience of admirers. Since he is assumed to be Dexter, he finds himself in the position of having to comment on Dexter's works, on which (as the author himself) he is theoretically a specialist—even though he has, in fact, neither written nor read them.

∿

Martins's situation is especially complex in that the other Dexter dwells in a region of literature that is totally foreign to him, an author of popular novels. So alien is this world that Martins is not only completely incapable of answering the audience's questions, but for the most part incapable of even understanding them: "Martin missed the first question altogether," Greene writes, "but luckily Crabbin filled the gap and answered it satisfactorily."[4]

To make matters even worse, Martins is not dealing with just any group of readers, but with a circle of admirers—literary enthusiasts of "his" works, who, delighted finally to have Dexter at their disposal and eager to pay homage, cannot resist showing off by asking highly specialized questions:

---

4. Graham Greene, *The Third Man* (London: Heinemann, 1950), p. 83.

A kind-faced woman in a hand-knitted jumper said wistfully, "Don't you agree, Mr. Dexter, that no one, no one has written about *feelings* so poetically as Virginia Woolf? In prose, I mean."

Crabbin whispered, "You might say something about the stream of consciousness."

"Stream of what?"[5]

Even on the question of writers that have influenced his work, Martins quickly finds himself in trouble. While there are certainly great masters whom he admires, he places himself within an entirely different lineage than the man who shares his name, a lineage featuring writers of dime-store fiction:

"Mr. Dexter, could you tell us what author has chiefly influenced you?"

Martins, without thinking, said, "Grey." He meant of course the author of *Riders of the Purple Sage*,[6] and he was pleased to find his reply gave general satisfaction— to all save an elderly Austrian who asked, "Grey. What Grey? I do not know the name."

Martins felt he was safe now and said, "Zane Grey— I don't know any other," and was mystified at the low subservient laughter from the English colony.[7]

---

5. Ibid., p. 86.
6. UB++.
7. Greene, op. cit., pp. 83–84.

No matter how Martins responds, it evidently has no direct impact on the discussion, which continues to follow its normal course. The dialogue transpires in a setting that seems not real, but rather like the space in dreams—possessed of its own laws, which are considerably removed from those that govern our ordinary conversations.

~

All the same, Crabbin senses that Martins is in trouble and finally steps in. But his intervention has the involuntary effect of complicating the exchange still further, by compounding the misunderstanding between the audience and the author:

> "That is a little joke of Mr. Dexter's. He meant the poet Gray—a gentle, mild, subtle genius—one can see the affinity."
>
> "And he is called Zane Grey?"
>
> "That was Mr. Dexter's joke. Zane Grey wrote what we call Westerns—cheap popular novelettes about bandits and cowboys."
>
> "He is not a great writer?"
>
> "No, no. Far from it," Mr. Crabbin said. "In the strict sense I would not call him a writer at all."[8]

Now, in saying this, Crabbin creates an intolerable situation for Martins, for he is taking on that sector of literature

---

8. Ibid., p. 84.

that constitutes Martins's personal universe and is his reason for living. And while in general Martins does not consider himself a writer, he becomes one upon seeing himself publicly denied that title:

> Martins told me that he felt the first stirrings of revolt at that statement. He had never regarded himself before as a writer; but Crabbin's self-confidence irritated him—even the way the light flashed back from Crabbin's spectacles seemed an added cause of vexation. Crabbin said, "He was just a popular entertainer."
>
> "Why the hell not?" Martins said fiercely.
>
> "Oh well, I merely meant—"
>
> "What was Shakespeare?"[9]

The situation quickly becomes even more tangled, because Crabbin, trying to come to the rescue of a writer who hasn't read the work he's discussing (because he hasn't written it), puts himself in a parallel situation. He, too, is reduced to speaking about books he doesn't know, as Martins is quick to point out:

> "Have you ever read Zane Grey?"
>
> "No, I can't say—"
>
> "Then you don't know what you are talking about."[10]

---

9. Ibid.
10. Ibid., p. 85.

This is unarguably true. Still, Crabbin is basing his judgment on Grey's place in the collective library that allows us to develop our idea of books. Based on the genre Grey's novels fall into, their titles, and what Martins communicates about them, Crabbin is no less justified in voicing an opinion than all the other informed non-readers we have encountered thus far.

~

Despite the occasional murmurs of surprise from his audience, Martins emerges quite gracefully from this exercise, for two reasons.

The first is the unfailing self-assurance he demonstrates, no matter what question is asked:

"And James Joyce, where would you put James Joyce, Mr. Dexter?"

"What do you mean, 'put'? I don't want to put anyone anywhere," Martins said. It had been a very full day: he had drunk too much with Colonel Cooler; he had fallen in love; a man had been murdered—and now he had the quite unjust feeling that he was being got at. Zane Grey was one of his heroes: he was damned if he was going to stand any nonsense.

"I mean would you put him among the really great?"

"If you want to know, I've never heard of him. What did he write?"[11]

---

11. Ibid.

If Martins's confidence is due in part to his character, it is also a function of his having been placed in a position of authority by the organizer of this meeting and his audience. Anything he might say redounds in his favor, since given the symbolic place he holds (and so long as his identity is not revealed), it is impossible that he would say anything foolish. Thus the more he demonstrates that he doesn't know his subject, the more convincing he becomes on another level:

> He didn't realize it, but he was making an enormous impression. Only a great writer could have taken so arrogant, so original a line. Several people wrote Zane Grey's name on the backs of envelopes and the Gräfin whispered hoarsely to Crabbin, "How do you spell Zane?"
>
> "To tell you the truth, I'm not quite sure."
>
> A number of names were simultaneously flung at Martins—little sharp pointed names like Stein, round pebbles like Woolf. A young Austrian with an intellectual black forelock called out, "Daphne du Maurier," and Mr. Crabbin winced and looked sideways at Martins. He said in an undertone, "Be gentle with them."[12]

Authority is an essential element at play in our discussions of books, if only because citing a text is most often a way of establishing one's own authority or contesting that of others.

---

12. Ibid., pp. 85–86.

Martins can connect Benjamin Dexter to the tradition of the western without risk of contradiction: either his statements will be accepted as illuminating and original, or, should they push the envelope too far, they will be understood as humorous.[13] In either case, the belief that his statement is accurate precedes its formulation, and thus the content of the statement is of relatively little importance.

To uncover and study the power in play, or, if you prefer, to analyze the exact position we find ourselves in when speaking about a work, is essential to our reflection on books we haven't read. It is only through such analysis that we will be able to adopt the correct strategy when we find ourselves in the position of not having read the books we're talking about, as Martins experiences here. We will have occasion to return to this question of strategy further on.

∾

In this public lecture, then, a writer who has not read the books on which he is expected to speak confronts an audience that

---

13. Before arriving in Vienna, Martins makes a stop in Frankfurt, where he is also mistaken for the other Dexter and where his frank answers are also taken to be humorous:

A man he could recognize from twenty feet away as a journalist approached his table.

"You Mr. Dexter?" he asked.

"Yes," Martins said, taken off his guard.

"You look younger than your photographs," the man said [. . .] "What about views on the American novel?"

"I don't read them."

"The well-known acid humor," the journalist said. (Ibid., p. 13.)

has not read those he has written. We have before us a perfect example of what is conventionally called a *dialogue of the deaf*.[14]

While this scenario is taken to the extreme in the case of the lecture in *The Third Man*, it occurs more commonly than you might think in our conversations about books. First, often the various interlocutors will not have read the book they are talking about, or will only have skimmed it, in which case they are each actually talking about a different book.

Second, in the more unusual case in which each person has held the book in his or her hands and truly knows it, the discussion is less about the book itself than about a fragmentary and reconstituted object (as we have seen in Umberto Eco, for example), a private screen book unrelated to the screen books of the other readers and unlikely, as a result, to overlap with them.

But what is at stake here transcends the case of any individual book. The dialogue of the deaf is a function not only of the divergence between the two authors Martins is speaking about, but also of the fact that the parties present are attempting to conduct a dialogue on the basis of two sets of books, or, if you prefer, two distinct and adversarial libraries. It is not simply two books that are in play, but two irreconcilable lists of names (Dexter and Dexter, Grey and Gray), as a result of the profound difference, indeed the incompatibility, of the two cultures confronting each other.

We might use the term *inner library* to characterize that set of books—a subset of the collective library—around which every

---

14. Concerning this notion, see my *Enquête sur Hamlet: Le dialogue de sourds* (Paris: Minuit, 2002), FB–.

personality is constructed, and which then shapes each person's individual relationship to books and to other people.[15] Specific titles figure in these private libraries, but, like Montaigne's, they are primarily composed of fragments of forgotten and imaginary books through which we apprehend the world.

In this case, the dialogue of the deaf arises from the fact that the inner libraries of Martins and of his audience don't overlap, or do so only to a limited extent. The conflict is not limited to any particular book, even if certain titles are mentioned, but bears more broadly on the very conception of what a book, and literature, may be. For this reason, achieving communication between the two libraries will not be easy, and any attempt to do so will inevitably create tension.

$\sim$

Thus it is that in truth we never talk about a book unto itself; a whole set of books always enters the discussion through the portal of a single title, which serves as a temporary symbol for a complete conception of culture. In every such discussion, our inner libraries—built within us over the years and housing all our secret books—come into contact with the inner libraries of others, potentially provoking all manner of friction and conflict.

For we are more than simple shelters for our inner libraries; we *are* the sum of these accumulated books. Little by

---

15. The second of the three libraries I am introducing in this book, the *inner library* is a subjective part of the *collective library* and includes the books that have left a deep impression on each subject.

little, these books have made us who we are, and they cannot be separated from us without causing us suffering. Just as Martins cannot bear to hear criticism of the novels written by his heroes, comments that challenge the books in our inner libraries, attacking what has become a part of our identity, may wound us to the core of our being.

Encounters with Professors

(in which we confirm, along with the Tiv tribe
of western Africa, that it is wholly unnecessary
to have opened a book in order to deliver
an enlightened opinion on it, even if you
displease the specialists in the process)

AS A TEACHER, it is my lot more often than average to find
myself obligated to speak to a large audience about books I
haven't read, either in the strict sense (having never opened
them) or the attenuated sense (having only skimmed them or
forgotten them). I am not sure I have dealt with the situation
any better than Rollo Martins. But I have often attempted to
reassure myself with the thought that those who are listening
to me are no doubt on similar ground and are probably no
more confident about it than I am.

I have observed over the years that this situation in no way
unsettles my students, who often comment about books they
haven't read in ways that are not only relevant, but indeed
quite accurate, by relying on elements of the text that I have,
involuntarily or not, conveyed to them. To avoid embarrassing

anyone in my place of employment, I shall choose an example that is geographically remote, to be sure, but close to our subject: that of the Tiv tribe of West Africa.

∽

If the Tiv are not comparable to students in general, a group of them did find themselves in such a position when an anthropologist named Laura Bohannan undertook to acquaint them with that classic entry in the English theatrical canon *Hamlet*,[1] which they had never heard of.

The choice of Shakespeare's play was not entirely disinterested. In response to a British colleague who suspected that Americans did not understand Shakespeare, Laura Bohannan, who is American, had countered that human nature is the same everywhere; he challenged her to prove it. Thus she left for Africa with a copy of *Hamlet* in her luggage, in the hope of demonstrating that human beings are fundamentally the same across cultural differences.

Welcomed by the tribe, with whom she had stayed once before, Laura Bohannan set up camp within the territory of a knowledgeable elder, who presided over some 140 people all more or less related to him. The anthropologist had hoped to be able to discuss the meaning of their ceremonies with her hosts, but most of their time was taken up with drinking beer. Isolated in her hut, she devoted herself to reading Shakespeare's play and eventually came up with an interpretation that seemed to her to be universal.

---

1. SB and HB++.

But the Tiv noticed that Laura Bohannan was spending a great deal of time reading the same text and, intrigued, suggested that she recount to them this story that seemed to fascinate her so much. They asked her to supply them with the necessary explanations as she went along and promised to be indulgent about her linguistic errors. She was thus given an ideal opportunity to verify her hypothesis and prove the universality of Shakespeare's play.

∼

It is not long before problems arise. In describing the beginning of the play, Bohannan tries to explain how, one night, three men standing guard outside a chief's compound suddenly see the dead chief approaching them. This is the first source of disagreement, because for the Tiv, there is no way the shape perceived by the men can be the dead leader:

> "Why was he no longer their chief?"
>
> "He was dead," I explained. "That is why they were troubled and afraid when they saw him."
>
> "Impossible," began one of the elders, handing his pipe on to his neighbor, who interrupted, "Of course it wasn't the dead chief. It was an omen sent by a witch. Go on."[2]

Shaken by the self-assurance of her interlocutors, Bohannan nonetheless continues her tale and recounts how Horatio

---

2. "Shakespeare in the Bush," *Natural History*, August/September 1966. On the Web: http://www.fieldworking.com/library/bohannan.html.

addresses Hamlet the elder to ask him what must be done to give him peace, and how, when the deceased fails to respond, he declares that it is up to the son of the dead chief, Hamlet, to intervene. At this there is a new stir of surprise in Bohannan's audience, since for the Tiv this kind of matter is not the business of the young, but of the elders, and the deceased has a living brother, Claudius:

> The old men muttered: such omens were matters for chiefs and elders, not for youngsters; no good could come of going behind a chief's back; clearly Horatio was not a man who knew things.[3]

Bohannan is then further disconcerted by finding herself unable to say whether Hamlet the elder and Claudius had the same mother, a distinction that is crucial in the eyes of the Tiv:

> "Did Hamlet's father and uncle have one mother?"
>
> His question barely penetrated my mind; I was too upset and thrown too far off balance by having one of the most important elements of Hamlet knocked straight out of the picture. Rather uncertainly I said that I thought they had the same mother, but I wasn't sure—the story didn't say. The old man told me severely that these genealogical details made all the difference and that when I got home I must ask the elders

---

3. Ibid.

about it. He shouted out the door to one of his younger wives to bring his goatskin bag.[4]

Bohannan then turns the discussion to Hamlet's mother, Gertrude, but this goes no better. Whereas in Western readings of the play, it is customary to insist on the slightly indecent rapidity with which Gertrude remarries after the death of her husband, the Tiv are surprised that she waited so long:

> "The son Hamlet was very sad because his mother had married again so quickly. There was no need for her to do so, and it is our custom for a widow not to go to her next husband until she has mourned for two years."
>
> "Two years is too long," objected the wife, who had appeared with the old man's battered goatskin bag. "Who will hoe your farms for you while you have no husband?"
>
> "Hamlet," I retorted without thinking, "was old enough to hoe his mother's farms himself. There was no need for her to remarry." No one looked convinced. I gave up.[5]

∽

If Bohannan finds it difficult to explain Hamlet's family situation to the Tiv, this is even more the case in getting them to

---

4. Ibid.
5. Ibid.

understand the place of ghosts in Shakespeare's play and the society that produced it:

> I decided to skip the soliloquy. Even if Claudius was here thought quite right to marry his brother's widow, there remained the poison motif, and I knew they would disapprove of fratricide. More hopefully I resumed, "That night Hamlet kept watch with the three who had seen his dead father. The dead chief again appeared, and although the others were afraid, Hamlet followed his dead father off to one side. When they were alone, Hamlet's dead father spoke."
>
> "Omens can't talk!" The old man was emphatic.
>
> "Hamlet's dead father wasn't an omen. Seeing him might have been an omen, but he was not." My audience looked as confused as I sounded. "It was Hamlet's dead father. It was a thing we call a 'ghost.' "[6]

As familiar as ghosts are to us, the Tiv do not believe in them and they have no place in their culture:

> I had to use the English word, for unlike many of the neighboring tribes, these people didn't believe in the survival after death of any individuating part of the personality.
>
> "What is a 'ghost'? An omen?"
>
> "No, a 'ghost' is someone who is dead but who

---

6. Ibid.

walks around and can talk, and people can hear him and
see him but not touch him."

They objected. "One can touch zombis."

"No, no! It was not a dead body the witches had animated to sacrifice and eat. No one else made Hamlet's
dead father walk. He did it himself."[7]

This explanation resolves the problem not at all, since the
Tiv are more rational than Anglo-Saxons and do not accept
the idea of the walking dead:

> "Dead men can't walk," protested my audience as
> one man.
>
> I was quite willing to compromise. "A 'ghost' is the
> dead man's shadow."
>
> But again they objected. "Dead men cast no shadows."
>
> "They do in my country," I snapped.
>
> The old man quelled the babble of disbelief that
> arose immediately and told me with that insincere, but
> courteous, agreement one extends to the fancies of the
> young, ignorant, and superstitious, "No doubt in your
> country the dead can also walk without being zom-
> bis." From the depths of his bag he produced a with-
> ered fragment of kola nut, bit off one end to show it
> wasn't poisoned, and handed me the rest as a peace of-
> fering.[8]

---

7. Ibid.
8. Ibid.

And despite all the concessions Bohannan makes, the whole play parades by without her succeeding at all in bridging the cultural distance to the Tiv and constructing, based on Shakespeare's play, a discursive object that she and they can share.

~

Even if they've never read a line of *Hamlet*, the Tiv are thus able to gain a number of specific ideas about the play, and so, like my students who haven't read the text I'm lecturing on, they find themselves perfectly capable of discussing it and offering their opinions.

Indeed, if the play offers a good occasion for the expression of their ideas, these ideas are neither simultaneous nor subsequent to it and thus do not, at the end of the day, need it at all. Their ideas are instead actually *prior*, in the sense that they constitute a whole and systematic vision of the world, in which the book is received and given a place.

In fact it is not even the book that is received, but those fragments of the book that circulate in every conversation or written commentary and come to substitute for it in its absence. What the Tiv end up speaking about is an imaginary *Hamlet*. And despite her being better informed about Shakespeare's play, Laura Bohannan's version is caught up in its own organized set of representations, and thus is no more real than theirs.

I propose the term *inner book* to designate the set of mythic representations, be they collective or individual, that come between the reader and any new piece of writing, shaping his reading without his realizing it. Largely unconscious, this imaginary book acts as a filter and determines the reception of new texts by selecting which of its elements will be retained and how they will be interpreted.[9]

As can be seen clearly in the case of the Tiv, the inner book contains one or more foundational stories that have an essential value for its bearer, particularly since they speak to him about origins and endings. Bohannan's reading of Shakespeare clashes with the theories on origins and survival that are contained in the collective inner book of the Tiv and that serve to bind the group together.

It is not, then, the story of *Hamlet* that they hear, but whatever in that story conforms to their notions of the family and the status of the dead and might serve to comfort them. In the places where the book does not conform to their expectations, the alarming passages are either ignored, or they undergo a transformation that allows the largest possible overlap between their inner book and *Hamlet*—or rather, not *Hamlet*,

---

9. The second of the three "books" studied in this essay, the *inner* book influences all the transformations to which we subject books, turning them into *screen books*. The term *inner book* appears in Proust with a meaning close to the one I am giving it: "As for the inner book of unknown symbols (symbols carved in relief they might have been, which my attention, as it explored my unconscious, groped for and stumbled against and followed the contours of, like a diver exploring the ocean-bed), if I tried to read them, no one could help me with any rules, for to read them was an act of creation in which no one can do our work for us or even collaborate with us [. . .] This book, more laborious to decipher than any other, is also the only one which has been dictated to us by reality, the only one of which the 'impression' has been printed in us by reality itself." *Time Regained, Remembrance of Things Past*, vol. 3, translated by C. K. Scott Moncrieff, Terence Kilmartin, and Andreas Mayor (New York: Random House, 1981), pp. 913–14.

but the image transmitted to them of Shakespeare's play through the prism of another inner book.

Since they are not discussing the work that Bohannan wants to talk to them about, the Tiv have no need for direct access to it. The references to *Hamlet* that the anthropologist manages to convey to them are sufficient to allow them to participate in a debate between two inner books—a debate in which Shakespeare's play serves both sides as, more than anything else, a pretext.

And since they are speaking primarily about their inner book, their comments on Shakespeare, like those of my students in similar circumstances, can very well begin before they acquire any knowledge of the work—which is itself, in any event, destined to melt and gradually disappear into the inner book.

∼

In the case of the Tiv, the inner book is more collective than individual. It is made up of general cultural representations that draw upon common ideas not only of family relations and the afterlife, but also of reading, how one appropriately approaches a book, and how, for example, to draw the line between reality and imagination.

We know nothing about the individual members of the Tiv, aside from their elderly leader, and it is plausible that the cohesion of the group tends to unify their reactions. But although a collective inner book would seem to exist for every culture, there also exists, for each member of the collective, an individual inner book, which is equally (if not more) active in the reception—which is to say, the construction—of cultural objects.

Woven from the fantasies and private mythologies particular to each person, the individual inner book is at work in our desire to read—that is, in the way we seek out and read books. It is that phantasmagorical object that every reader lives to pursue, of which the best books he encounters in his life will be but imperfect fragments, compelling him to continue reading.

We might further speculate that every writer is driven by the attempt to discover and give form to his inner book and is perpetually dissatisfied with the actual books he encounters, including his own, however polished they may be. How indeed might we begin to write, or continue doing so, without that ideal image of a perfect book—one congruent to ourselves, that is—which we endlessly seek and constantly approach, but never reach?

Like collective inner books, individual inner books create a system for receiving other texts and participate both in their reception and their reorganization. In this sense, they form a kind of grid through which we read the world, and books in particular, organizing the way we perceive these texts while producing the illusion of transparency.

It is these inner books that make our exchanges about books so difficult, rendering it impossible to establish unanimity about the object of discussion. They are part of what I have called, in my study of *Hamlet*, an *inner paradigm*—a system for perceiving reality that is so idiosyncratic that no two paradigms can truly communicate.[10]

---

10. *Enquête sur Hamlet.*

The existence of the inner book, along with unreading or forgetting, is what makes the way we discuss books so discontinuous and heterogeneous. What we take to be the books we have read is in fact an anomalous accumulation of fragments of texts, reworked by our imagination and unrelated to the books of others, even if these books are materially identical to ones we have held in our hands.

∾

That what the Tiv offer is, to say the least, a partial reading of a book they have not read should not lead us to believe either that their reading is a caricature—for it underscores the characteristics of every act of reading—or that it is without interest. Quite to the contrary, the double exteriority of the Tiv in relation to Shakespeare's work (they haven't read it and they are from a different culture) places them in a privileged position to discuss it.

In refusing to believe in the ghost story, they approach the position of a minority trend—but an active one—in Shakespearean criticism, which casts doubt on the reappearance of Hamlet's father and suggests that the hero may have been suffering hallucinations.[11] The hypothesis is heterodox, but is at the least deserving of examination, a circumstance facilitated in this case by the foreignness of the Tiv to the play. Not knowing the text—in two different ways—paradoxically gives them more direct access, not, to be sure, to its supposed universal truth, but to one of its many potential riches.

---

11. Ibid.

Thus, to return to the situation I mentioned at the beginning of this chapter, it is not astonishing that my students, without having read the book I am discussing, quickly grasp certain of its elements and feel free to comment on it, based on their cultural notions and personal history. And it is also unsurprising that their comments—however far removed from the initial text (but what, in fact, might it mean to be *close*?)—bring to the encounter an originality that they would undoubtedly have lacked had they undertaken to read the book.

VII

Encounters with the Writer

(in which Pierre Siniac demonstrates that it may
be important to watch what you say in the
presence of a writer, especially when he himself
hasn't read the book whose author he is)

WHEN YOU DO NOT necessarily know the book you're talk-ing about, there is a person even worse to encounter than a teacher—the person at once the most interested in your opinion of a particular book, and the most likely to know whether you are telling the truth about having read it. This person is the author of the book, who is assumed a priori to have read the book himself.

One might think that you would have to have a stroke of incredible bad luck to find yourself in such a situation. In-deed, many people spend a whole lifetime of non-reading without encountering a single writer, never mind the excep-tional case of the author of a book they haven't read while pretending the contrary.

But everything depends on your professional context. Lit-erary critics regularly come into contact with writers—all the more so, of course, in that the two groups overlap. Given that both groups often include the same people, critics move within a world so insular that in commenting on a book, they have hardly any other choice than to praise it to the skies.

Such is also the case, to my misfortune, with university professors. Very few of my colleagues, in fact, do not publish and do not feel obliged to send me their books. Every year I thus find myself in the delicate situation of giving my opinion to authors who know their own texts and who are, moreover, experienced critics, skilled in evaluating to what extent I have actually read the books, and to what extent I am bluffing.

~

The public remarks about books made by the two heroes of *Ferdinaud Céline*,[1] Pierre Siniac's celebrated thriller, might best be described with the word *ambiguous*. In the opening pages of the novel, Dochin and Gastinel, the two authors of the best seller *La Java brune*,[2] appear as guests on a literary television program and behave rather strangely, to say the least, in their exchanges with the host. It is as though they both prefer not to answer the questions they are being asked about a book that ought to be a source of nothing but joy for them, since it has earned them a fortune and gotten them invited on television.

---

1. SB+.
2. UB−.

The younger and physically slighter of the two authors, Jean-Rémi Dochin, seems manifestly ill at ease during the broadcast:

> Dochin, for his part, seemed more and more to be falling asleep, completely out of it. He seemed to be having trouble following. Before the cameras, he seemed hesitant, uncomfortable, almost never completing the few sentences he managed to say.[3]

It turns out Dochin has an excellent reason to appear, in the narrator's words, "more than at sea"[4] on the subject of his own book. He has been dispossessed of the book that he has supposedly cowritten by Gastinel, who is as physically imposing as his companion is slender, and who has forced his own name onto the cover with Dochin's.

Originally approached by the writer Dochin as a possible publisher, Gastinel read the manuscript and immediately became convinced he had a huge success on his hands; he became determined to put his own name on the book as coauthor, despite not having written a word. To force Dochin to consent, Gastinel decided to blackmail him. With this goal in mind, he seduced a girl at a dance, then took her to his country house along with Dochin, whom he got drunk. After raping the young woman and running her over with his car, he filmed Dochin bending over her corpse, on which he had discreetly planted the writer's ID.

---

3. Pierre Siniac, *Ferdinaud Céline* (Paris: Rivages/noir, 2002), p. 18.
4. Ibid., p. 20.

Based on a tape closely guarded by Gastinel, Dochin is thus under constant threat of being accused of a murder he didn't commit, but which he allowed to happen without intervening. He finds himself forced to abide by the wishes of his blackmailer, who has, in exchange for his silence, appropriated the right to be credited as coauthor of the book and to pocket half the royalties.

≈

Though neither laying claim to another writer's manuscript nor committing a murder seems to pose much of a moral problem to Gastinel, he is nonetheless uncomfortable at the thought of speaking about the book to a large audience. He has therefore exacted a pledge from the program's host not to mention the contents of the book, a promise of which Gastinel reminds him as soon as the questions get specific enough to present a threat:

> "Don't forget the little deal we made before the program. Dochin and I do not in any way want to give away the plot of our novel. So, if you don't mind, let's talk about the authors instead. At bottom, I think that's what your viewers are interested in anyway."[5]

Gastinel's behavior is even more surprising in that he is quite eloquent on the subject of the duo's follow-up book,

5. Ibid., p. 11.

the as yet unwritten sequel to *La Java brune*, to the point of publicly recounting several of its episodes. What is clearly out of the question, at least in the presence of Dochin, is for Gastinel to speak about Dochin's work.

As it turns out, Gastinel's discretion is completely justified. That he prefers not to speak about the book is not due to not having read it, like many other characters we have encountered; it is because Dochin, who is nevertheless the book's author, has not read it. In effect, Siniac's novel constructs an unlikely situation in which one supposed coauthor is speaking about a book he has read without having written it, while the other is speaking about a book he has written but hasn't read.

To truly understand the situation in which the two characters find themselves during this first scene, the reader must know that Dochin is not the victim of just one trap—Gastinel's blackmail to appropriate royalties—but of two, the second of which is revealed only in the novel's final pages and which illuminates it retrospectively. Whereas the first trap explains Dochin's strange attitude, only in discovering the second one do we come to understand Gastinel's.

While he was working on the manuscript of *Java brune*, Dochin, who at the time had no permanent address, was taken in by Céline Ferdinaud, the madam of a seedy hotel. Having barely begun to read the text, Céline was overcome with enthusiasm and urged Dochin to complete and publish it. She even offered to help on a practical level, by retyping the poorly typed pages that Dochin gave her each day.

The problem is that Céline seized the opportunity of this secretarial work to write a completely different novel, which she gradually substituted for Dochin's, retaining only the title, the period during which the story took pace, and the first names of the two child protagonists. Day by day, she replaced Dochin's poorly written and unpublishable pages with a much more carefully composed text of her own.

What is the point of this stratagem? The name Céline Ferdinaud is in fact an alias for a notorious collaborator in the Occupation, Céline Feuhant. With an eye to blackmailing a number of prominent fellow collaborators who had peacefully resumed their lives, Céline had decided to publish her fictionalized memoirs. But at the Liberation she had agreed, in exchange for a promise of impunity, to desist from calling attention to herself. Unable to publish the book as it was lest she be recognized, she discovered her lodger's third-rate manuscript and hit upon the idea of publishing her own book under his name, without the author—if we can call him that—realizing it.

Thus two texts bearing the same title continually circulate throughout Siniac's novel, each by turns substituting for the other. Dochin, like the reader, fails to understand how his own text—which he quite rightly judges to be execrable— could have aroused the enthusiasm of the entire critical community, which has, in fact, been given the other manuscript, written by Céline. For the duration of the ruse, then, Gastinel, who is in on the plot, is inclined to remain as vague as possible when speaking of the book in Dochin's presence, so that Dochin will not find out that the book causing all the excitement is one he has never read.

∽

Dochin thus finds himself in the position of having to speak about a book that is unknown to him, although he believes himself to be its author. Unlike Rollo Martins, who knew that he was not speaking about the same author as the members of his audience, Dochin has no idea he is participating in a dialogue of the deaf, since Gastinel is doing his best (failing to give him a copy of his book, among other measures) to prevent Dochin from discovering that *La Java brune* is not *La Java brune*.

It is essential for Gastinel—who has read the same book as his audience, but who must at any cost prevent his partner from being too explicit, lest the host's reaction tip Dochin off to the substitution of the manuscript—that the comments made during the broadcast be as ambiguous as possible. One of his solutions is to insist on speaking of something other than the text, such as the lives of the authors or their next book.

Another option for Gastinel is to make sure that the discussion touches only on the few superficial aspects of the text that are shared by the two books. This is the case for the Occupation period that serves as a backdrop for both works, as well as for the two child heroes, Max and Mimile, whom Céline has made sure to retain in her version of *La Java brune*:

> [The host] came charging back: he was dying, it was clear, to talk about the novel. Gastinel rebuffed him, then consented, all the same, after emitting a declamatory sigh, to say two or three words on the work [. . .] It was thus agreed to say two or three little things—which

were not at all compromising, there was still this obsession with not giving away the plot—about the Max and Mimile characters, whereupon the portly author directed the discussion authoritatively, as though he himself were the host of the discussion, to the Occupation in Paris in general, the raids, the restrictions, the lines in front of the poorly stocked shops, the curfew, the lists of hostages posted on the walls, the anonymous denunciations, and the entire litany of daily miseries of those four interminable years. There was nothing inappropriate in doing so, besides, since this oppressive, lugubrious atmosphere was the constant backdrop for the book.[6]

For Gastinel, these generalities about the two children or the setting shared by the two works are the only safe territory. On the few occasions when the conversation does become less vague, incomprehension starts to blossom between Dochin and the program host, and Gastinel is obliged to intervene, offering comments that are ambiguous enough to set both parties at ease:

"You're going to make yourself enemies."

"So much the better—we love a good fight. In any event, since our success we've already had our share. We've even turned away a few."

"The references to . . . certain people in prominence at the time . . . go pretty far, at moments . . ."

6. Ibid., p. 17.

"That's not at all my opinion," said Dochin. "You must have misread."

"We never really attack people," said Gastinel. "No more than, say, a few discreet jabs."[7]

The problem facing Gastinel is that he has to find phrases simultaneously befitting the book Dochin has read—the one he wrote—with which the program host is unfamiliar, and the book that the host has in his hands, whose existence is unknown to Dochin. Whereas Dochin's manuscript shows no interest in complicating matters for newly respectable ex-collaborators, Céline's is a full-blown attack on her former accomplices. The expression "discreet jabs" is a compromise formation, in the Freudian sense, between the two books being discussed simultaneously on the program. So it is that live, in front of millions of viewers, Gastinel finds himself compiling fragments of a joint book that might offer an acceptable reconciliation to both parties, within which each reader will be able to identify his own text.

≈

But the television host is not the only one experiencing difficulties in having a coherent conversation with Dochin. The same holds for Céline and for other critics, who talk to him constantly about a book in which he finds it hard to recognize himself.

---

7. Ibid., p. 23.

If Céline, to her misfortune, is familiar with Dochin's book, having been obliged to type it out daily, she can't tell him what she really thinks of it and is forced to talk to him about an imaginary book that he has difficulty superimposing onto his own. He is stupefied by Céline's wildly enthusiastic observations during the period when she is transcribing the manuscript, remarks that understandably seem a bit off the mark to him in that she is really addressing herself:

"Frankly, this is a lucky time for me. It's so hard to find a good writer, especially these days. All the great ones have taken leave . . . and never returned! 'I leave you my books—enjoy!' Céline . . . Aragon . . . Giono . . . Beckett . . . Henry Miller . . . Not to mention Marcel [. . .] And when I think that there are crossed out sentences that can no longer even be deciphered because you've drenched everything with strokes of your pen! When by some miracle I manage to read what you've slashed out, I'm dumbfounded. You've eliminated true gems! I start wondering what you could possibly have been thinking when you got rid of all that."

The smile beginning to form on my lips must have expressed an outraged skepticism.

"One small question: are you sure you read my manuscript?"[8]

What is being described in this passage to the point of caricature is an experience familiar to all writers, in which they

---

8. Ibid., p. 81.

realize that what is said about their books does not correspond to what they believe they have written. Every writer
who has conversed at any length with an attentive reader, or
read an article of any length about himself, has had the un-
canny experience of discovering the absence of any connection between what he meant to accomplish and what has
been grasped of it. There is nothing astonishing in this dis-
juncture; since their inner books differ by definition, the one
the reader has superimposed on the book is unlikely to seem
familiar to the writer.

This experience is unpleasant enough with a reader who
has not understood your book's project, but it is perhaps paradoxically more painful when the reader is well-intentioned
and appreciates the book and grows passionate when he begins talking about it in detail. In his enthusiasm, he resorts to
the words most familiar to him, and instead of this bringing
him closer to the writer's book, it brings him closer to his
own ideal book, which is so crucial to his relation to language
and to others that it is unique, and not transcribable into any
other words. In this case, the author's disillusionment may be
even more pronounced, since it arises from the discovery of
the unfathomable distance that separates us from others.

It might then be said that the chances of wounding an author by speaking about his book are all the greater when we
love it. Beyond the general expressions of satisfaction that
tend to create a sense of common ground, there is every likelihood that trying to be more precise in our exposition of
why we appreciated the book will be demoralizing for him.
In the attempt, we force him into an abrupt confrontation
with everything that is irreducible in the other, and thus irre-

ducible in him and in the words through which he has attempted to express himself.

In Siniac's book, this painful experience of incomprehension is heightened by the real dissociation between the book
the writer believes he has written and the one the others believe they have read, since in this instance there are two materially distinct books. But beyond the surface intrigue, it is
indeed this crisis of impossible communication between the
writer's inner book and those of his readers that is played out
here, in an almost allegorical manner.

It's unsurprising, therefore, that the question of the double
is such an obsession in Siniac's novel. Dochin is a participant
in a process of doubling in that he does not recognize himself
in what others say about his book, just as other people's comments often make writers feel that they are dealing with a
text that is *other* (which is effectively the case). The doubling
is produced by the presence in us of the inner book, which
can be transmitted to no one and superimposed on no other.
For the inner book, the manifestation of everything that
makes us absolutely unique is the expression within us of the
incommunicable itself.[9]

∽

What, then, are we to do when facing the writer himself?
The case of the encounter with the author of a book we

9. The author of neither the book he wrote nor of Gastinel's crime, Dochin
will also end up taking responsibility, under duress, for the murder of Céline,
committed by the French secret service.

haven't read at first seems to be the thorniest case, since the author is assumed to be familiar with what he wrote, but it is revealed in the end to be the simplest of all.

First, it is far from evident, despite what you would expect, that the writer is in the best position either to speak about his book or to remember it precisely. The example of Montaigne, unable to identify the cases in which he is being quoted, serves as evidence that after we write a text and are separated from it, we may be as far from it as others are.

But second and most especially, if it is true that the inner books of two individuals cannot coincide, it is useless to plunge into long explanations when faced with a writer. His anxiety is likely to grow as we discuss what he has written, along with his sense that we are talking to him about another book or that we have the wrong person. And he is even in danger of undergoing a genuine experience of depersonalization, confronted as he is with the enormity of what separates one individual from another.

As may be seen, there is only one sensible piece of advice to give to those who find themselves having to talk to an author about one of his books without having read it: praise it without going into detail. An author does not expect a summary or a rational analysis of his book and would even prefer you not to attempt such a thing. He expects only that, while maintaining the greatest possible degree of ambiguity, you will tell him that you like what he wrote.

VIII

Encounters with Someone You Love

(in which we see, along with Bill Murray and his
groundhog, that the ideal way to seduce someone
by speaking about books he or she loves
without having read them yourself would
be to bring time to a halt)

CAN WE IMAGINE two beings so close that their inner books come, at least for a while, to coincide? Our last example of literary confrontation brings up quite another kind of risk from that of appearing to be an impostor in the eyes of a book's author: that of being unable to seduce the person you have fallen for, because of not having read the books he or she likes.

It is a commonplace to say that our sentimental life is deeply marked by books, from childhood onward. First of all, fictional characters exert a great deal of influence over our choices in love by representing inaccessible ideals to which we try to make others conform, usually without success. But more subtly, too, the books we love offer a sketch of a whole universe that we secretly inhabit, and in which we desire the other person to assume a role.

One of the conditions of happy romantic compatibility is, if not to have read the same books, to have read at least some books in common with the other person—which means, moreover, to have non-read the same books. From the beginning of the relationship, then, it is crucial to show that we can match the expectations of our beloved by making him or her sense the proximity of our inner libraries.

∾

It is a strange adventure indeed that befalls Phil Connors (played by Bill Murray), the hero of Harold Ramis's film *Groundhog Day*.[1] The star weatherman of a major American television station, Connors is sent in the dead of winter, accompanied by the program's producer, Rita (played by Andie MacDowell), and a cameraman, to cover an important event of American provincial life, Groundhog Day.

The day takes its name from a ceremony, widely reported in the media, that happens in the small town of Punxsutawney, Pennsylvania, every year on February 2. On that date, a groundhog named Phil (just like Phil Connors) is pulled from his hutch, and based on his reactions, it is determined whether the winter is about to end or will continue for six more weeks. The groundhog consultation ceremony

---

1. *Groundhog Day* (1993), directed by Harold Ramis, starring Bill Murray and Andie MacDowell.

is rebroadcast throughout the country, alerting the nation to whatever bad weather is in store.

Having arrived on the eve of the ceremony with his crew, Phil Connors spends the night in a bed-and-breakfast. The next morning, he goes to the spot where the segment is to be shot and provides his commentary on the behavior of the groundhog, which indicates that winter will continue. With little desire to steep in small-town life any longer than necessary, Phil Connors resolves to head back to Pittsburgh that very day, but the crew's vehicle gets stuck in a blizzard as they try to leave town, and the three journalists are forced to resign themselves to spending another night in Punxsutawney.

~

Everything begins for Phil the following morning, if that phrase makes any sense, since the following morning is exactly what fails to arrive. Awakened at six o'clock by the music of his alarm clock, Phil notices that the music is the same as that of the previous day, but is not particularly concerned. His anxiety begins when he realizes that the broadcast that follows is also identical to that of the day before, and that the scenes he is seeing from his window are those he saw a day earlier. And his uneasiness increases when, upon leaving his room, he runs into the same man as the day before, who greets him with the same words.

In this way, Phil gradually realizes that he is reliving the previous day. The remainder of the day is, in fact, an exact repetition of all the scenes he experienced twenty-four hours earlier. He encounters the same beggar asking him for money and is then approached by the same college friend—whom he hasn't seen in years, and who has now become an insurance salesman bent on selling him a policy—before stepping in the same puddle of water. And having arrived at the location where the groundhog ceremony is being filmed, he observes the same scene as the day before, in which Phil the groundhog delivers the same verdict.

During the third day of his stay in Punxsutawney, on hearing the same radio program for the third time as he awakes, Phil begins to realize that the temporal disorder plaguing him has not caused just one repetition, but that he is condemned to relive the same day eternally, without any hope of escaping either the small town or the time period that has enveloped it.

His entrapment is airtight, for even death has ceased to offer any deliverance. Resolved to put an end to the sequence of identical days, Phil, after consulting a physician and a psychoanalyst both unable to intervene in this unprecedented clinical case, despairingly kidnaps the other Phil (the groundhog), steals a car, and, during a police chase, hurls himself with the animal into a ravine—before waking the next morning to discover himself unharmed, in his bed, listening to the same radio program at dawn of the same day.

∽

This temporal disorder is the source of a whole series of highly original situations, and linguistic situations in particular. Present on two stages—that of the day itself and that of other identical days, past and future—Phil is free to play continually on the double meanings permitted by his immobility in time and, for example, to declare to the woman he loves, as he carves an ice sculpture of her face, that he has spent some time studying her.

If reliving the same day an infinite number of times has its inconveniences, the situation is not without its advantages. It allows you, for example, to perform actions that are possible only because of a detailed knowledge, right down to the split second, of the organization of each day. Hence Phil notices a moneybag left unattended for a few seconds in the back of an armored vehicle parked in front of a bank and, during that brief moment of inattention, makes off with it.

The situation also ensures total impunity, since Phil is certain that whatever he does, his crimes and misdemeanors will be expunged in the night. He can thus exceed the speed limit, drive his car on train tracks, and be arrested by the police without its making any difference, since he will wake up without any of those events having occurred.

A stoppage in time also allows you to use the strategy of trial and error. So, for instance, when Phil meets a young woman he finds attractive, he asks her to tell him her name, what high school she went to, and the name of her French teacher. When he runs into her again "the next day," he passes himself off as an old school friend and refers to their supposedly shared memories of adolescence, thus increasing the likelihood of a conquest.

≈

Having gradually fallen in love with Rita, the show's producer, Phil attempts to seduce her through the constantly improving technique accessible only to those whose actions are without consequence due to the eternal repetition of time. While having a drink with her one evening, he takes note of her favorite drink, so that he can deliberately order the same thing "next time." And after committing the error—one that is less than fatal only in this subset of space-time—of proposing a toast to Phil the groundhog, to the scorn of his beloved, who tells him frostily that she drinks only to world peace, he improves his performance "the next day" by proposing a toast befitting a true pacifist.

It is in the context of Phil's day-by-day perfection of himself as a romantic interest that the scene relevant to our inquiry occurs—a scene that shows the role unread books may play in the genesis of a love affair. After many days of practice, Phil has managed to have a conversation with Rita that she finds totally satisfying—and for good reason!—in which her suitor articulates, one by one, every sentence she dreams of hearing in an ideal world of love. He is thus able, for instance, despite his being happy only in cities, to mention in her presence his dream of living in the mountains, far from all civilization.

At this point, Phil suffers a moment of distraction and, forgetting to watch his words, makes a new mistake. In a moment of shared confidences, Rita confides to him that her college studies did not initially incline her toward a career in television, and when Phil asks for details, she tells him, "I studied nineteenth-century Italian poetry." Her response causes Phil to burst out laughing and blurt without thinking, "You must have had a lot of time on your hands!"—at which Rita gives him an icy look, and he realizes his blunder.

But there is nothing irreparable in this world in which everything always begins identically anew and in which mistakes can be rectified so quickly. The next time Phil hears Rita confess her passion for nineteenth-century Italian poetry—having ransacked the local library for material in the meantime, presumably—he is able to recite, with considerable pathos, excerpts from the libretto of *Rigoletto*,[2] as the young woman looks on admiringly. Forced to talk about books he hasn't read, all he has to do is to stretch the few seconds of his reply by one day, and he is able to comply perfectly with his beloved's desire.

Phil's attempt to seduce Rita goes beyond literature. Phil takes advantage of his halt in time to learn how to play the piano and goes faithfully to his lesson "every day." He has learned that Rita's ideal man plays a musical instrument. Based on intensive training during a single time slot that extends over days, he is able, one evening when Rita goes to a party with live music (as she does, by definition, every night), to appear with the band as a jazz musician.

∼

Conversely to our other examples, *Groundhog Day*'s complex narrative device allows it to play out a fantasy of completion and transparency in which we see two individuals communicate about books, and thus about themselves, without any sense of loss. Having the time to study the essential books of

---

2. FB++.

another person, to the point where we come to share the same ones, might perhaps be what is necessary to achieve a genuine exchange on cultural matters and a perfect overlap between the two inner books.

In the numerous situations where we find it necessary to charm another person, such a method might allow us to indicate to him or her that we share a common cultural universe. By training himself in Rita's preferred reading material and thus penetrating as deeply as possible into her private world, Phil is straining to create the illusion that their inner books are the same. And perhaps an ideal and deeply shared love should indeed give each lover access to the secret texts of which the other is composed.

But the images and fragments of text that are the stuff of our inner books are so singular to each of us that only through an indefinite extension of time might two inner books find communion—for to do so is to achieve a melding of two people's private worlds. In the slow-motion existence Phil is living, language is no longer an uninterrupted and ir-reversible flow, and it becomes possible, as in the scene of the toast to the groundhog, to stop at every sentence and exam-ine its origin and value, connecting it to the biography and inner life of the other.

Only such an artificial halting of time and language would allow someone else to reproduce the texts buried within us; in real life, these texts are caught up in an irresistible move-ment that transforms them constantly and renders all hope of overlap impossible. For if our inner books, like our fantasies, are relatively stable, the screen books about which we speak endlessly are perpetually being modified, as we shall see, and it is futile to imagine we can put a stop to their metamorphoses.

The fantasy of overlap can thus be staged only by way of recourse to the supernatural. As we have seen, most of the time our discussions with others about books are necessarily and unfortunately based on fragments reworked by our private fantasies, and hence on something quite different from the books written by writers, who in any case don't generally recognize themselves in what their readers say about them.

~

Beyond the humor of certain situations, there is something frightening in the way Phil sets out to seduce Rita, since it effectively suppresses the uncertainty that is normally part of communication. Endlessly telling the Other the words she wants to hear, being exactly the person she expects, is paradoxically to deny her as an other, since it amounts to no longer being a subject, fragile and uncertain, in her presence.

Since there is a moral in films, if not in life, it is not through his possession of Rita, but through his dispossession of himself, that Phil will finally achieve his ends. If the slow accumulation of the words awaited by the Other allows Phil to kiss Rita, getting the girl is not sufficient to set time back in motion; no matter how much progress he makes with his beloved, Phil continues to wake up on the same day.

But as time goes by and events repeat identically, Phil changes and loses his arrogance toward others. He begins to take an interest in them, to ask them questions about their lives, to do them favors. The days continue to repeat, but they are now devoted to helping others, with Phil using his method for personal improvement for benevolent purposes, such as preventing an old man from freezing to death in the street or catching a little boy who falls out of a tree.

In becoming interested in others, he himself becomes interesting, and he manages, through his kindness, to win Rita's heart in a single day. And after falling asleep alongside her in the room where he has been waking up every day without progressing in time, he has the surprise, one day, of reawakening to discover the young woman still with him and to hear, for the first time, different music streaming from his alarm clock. Thus does he manage at last to cross the border, in one unsurpassable moment, that separates his day from the days to come.

Ways of Behaving

Not Being Ashamed

(in which it is confirmed, with regard to the
novels of David Lodge, that the first condition
for speaking about a book you haven't
read is not to be ashamed)

WE NOW ARRIVE at this book's raison d'être: having detailed
the different modes of non-reading and studied several of the
situations in which the need to discuss unread books may occur, it is now time to discuss the various means of extricating
ourselves from these situations with grace. Some of these solutions have already been mentioned in preceding chapters or
derive logically from my remarks, but the moment has come
to examine the structure of these methods more closely.

As we have seen, talking about books has little to do with
reading. The two activities are completely separable; I for one
speak at greater length and with greater perception about
books that I have more or less stopped reading, which grants
me the necessary distance—Musil's overall perspective—to
speak about them accurately. The difference between talking
about books and reading them is a function of the fact that

the former implies a third party, whether present or absent. That implied third party has palpable effects on the act of reading as well, by suggesting that an outside presence might be able to change how our reading unfolds.

As I have attempted to show in the previous section through a number of concrete situations, our discussion of books is the stage for a conflict in which our relationship with the Other, whatever its nature may be, ultimately wins out over our relationship to the text—which is itself inevitably affected by the struggle.

∼

There is no doubt that teaching is one of the professions that exposes us most relentlessly to the obligation to comment on unread books. Almost all of us, in fact, find ourselves having to talk about books that we lack the time—or more simply, the desire—to read. And the risk is ever present of having to speak about a given text with the author himself, or with other specialists whom it is not easy to deceive.

A teacher himself and thus attuned to the habits of the profession, the English novelist David Lodge has reflected at least twice in his books about what attitude we should adopt with regard to books we haven't read. The two examples figure in two novels—*Changing Places*[1] and *Small World*[2]—that

---

1. SB+.
2. SB+.

explore the intellectual and sentimental worlds of an academic microcosm, novels that have helped to establish a specific literary genre known as the campus novel.

The first case, which occurs in *Small World*, involves a rather unusual dialogue. One of the denizens of this campus microcosm, Robin Dempsey, carries out a discussion with a computer he has borrowed, one so advanced that it can sustain a normal conversation. The machine, which answers to the name ELIZA and thus seems to be female, gradually becomes his most intimate confidant.

Having at last discovered someone to whom he can open his heart without fear of indiscretion, Dempsey confides to ELIZA the full fury and contempt he feels for one of his colleagues, Philip Swallow:

Robin Dempsey: I'm not feeling any better.

ELIZA: Why is that?

R.D.: This business about Philip Swallow.

ELIZA: Tell me about Philip Swallow.

R.D.: I already told you about him.

ELIZA: Is there anything you would like to add to your previous remarks?

R.D.: Swallow epitomizes the unfairness of life to me. At Rummidge he got the senior lectureship I should have got. Then he got the chair there by a lucky fluke. Now he's having a great success with this pathetic book about Hazlitt.[3]

---

3. *Small World: An Academic Romance* (New York: Macmillan, 1984), p. 247.

All those who believe themselves to have been the victim of injustice in their academic careers will understand Dempsey's anger. And they will recognize themselves even more in the lines that follow:

> ELIZA: Tell me about Hazlitt.
> R.D.: I'm not interested in Hazlitt. I haven't even read Swallow's rotten book. I don't need to. I sat through enough tedious examiners meetings with him to know what it's like. The idea of his being a serious candidate for the UNESCO Chair is preposterous.[4]

These lines represent quite accurately the kind of goodwill that tends to prevail in academic communities, particularly when it comes to evaluating our colleagues' work, which most often we haven't read anyway. Clearly, David Lodge is speaking about a world he knows well.

≈

Like Dempsey and a number of others in the academy, I have spent enough time in meetings with my colleagues to have an idea, be it positive or negative, of the value of their books without having to read them. Contrary to the celebrated Proustian argument dissociating the work from the author— or rather, contrary to a certain reading of that argument—a book is not a meteorite or the product of a hidden self. It is

---

4. Ibid.

often, more simply, an extension of the person we know (on the condition, obviously, that we take the trouble of getting to know him), and it is quite possible to forge an opinion of it, like Dempsey, merely by spending time with the author.

What Dempsey is saying here—and probably David Lodge as well, through him—is well known in circles where books are common. As we have established, it is not necessary to read a book to have a clear sense of it and to talk about it, not just in general terms but even in detail. For there is no such thing as an isolated book. A book is an element in the vast ensemble I have called the *collective library*, which we do not need to know comprehensively in order to appreciate any one of its elements (Dempsey, after all, has a keen sense of what *kind* of book he is dealing with). The trick is to define the book's place in that library, which gives it meaning in the same way a word takes on meaning in relation to other words.

We are never dealing with just the book in our hand, but with a set of books common to our particular culture, where any individual book in the set might be lacking. So there is no reason not to tell the truth: to acknowledge that we haven't read some specific element in the collective library, which in no way prevents us from having an overall view of the library and remaining one of its readers. It is the entire library that is called into play through each book, which serves as a kind of temporary shimmering prism through which we see the whole. Dempsey's view of his colleague's book is thus perfectly reasonable, as far as subjective opinions go, and it is unlikely that it would be noticeably different if he had taken the time to read it.

Besides the fact that the book in question is an element in

a larger ensemble, which provides Dempsey a certain amount of information to begin with, he knows enough about the book (through its title, his acquaintance with the author, what he has heard about it) to be able to judge whether it is of interest to him. It is the book's perceived affinities (or lack thereof) with his own inner book that allow him to make a judgment—affinities that are not directly detectable in Swallow's text and that probably would be neither reinforced nor diminished if Dempsey were to familiarize himself with it.

~

It should be the most normal of behaviors to acknowledge that we haven't read a book while nevertheless reserving the right to pass judgment on it. If we rarely see this practice in action, it is because acknowledging our non-reading (which, as we have seen, may be quite active rather than passive) is, in our culture, deeply and ineradicably marked by guilt.

It is striking that Dempsey only offers his opinion of Swallow's book so frankly because he is speaking to a computer, and not a living person. His attitude changes completely, moreover, as soon as he has the sense that his interlocutor is endowed with a kind of personality—that is, as soon as it emits what is theoretically impossible for a machine, an opinion:

R.D.: . . . The idea of his being a serious candidate for the UNESCO Chair is preposterous.
ELIZA: I wouldn't say that.

It is this last line of the dialogue that Robin Dempsey has been staring at, transfixed, for the last few minutes.

Its appearance made the hairs on the back of his neck
bristle, for it is of an entirely different order from anything ELIZA has produced until now: not a question,
not a request, not a statement about something already
mentioned in the discourse, but an expression of *opinion*. How can ELIZA have opinions? How can she
know anything about the UNESCO Chair that Robin
himself doesn't know, or hasn't told her? Robin is almost afraid to ask. At last, slowly and hesitantly, he types:

    What do you know about it?

Instantly ELIZA replies:

    More than you think.

Robin turns pale, then red. He types:

    All right, if you're so clever, tell me who will get the
UNESCO Chair.

Whereupon the machine, gradually freeing itself from its status as a machine, replies imperturbably, "Philip Swallow."[5]

If the computer is able to proffer firm opinions, including
its thoughts on the subject of future academic appointments,
it is because it is not as autonomous as Dempsey has long believed, but is being controlled from a distance by one of his
colleagues. The discovery of this ruse plunges Dempsey into
a fury—which is understandable, for in his ignorance that his
interlocutor is human he has revealed some of his most private thoughts, and specifically his hatred of Swallow, thus ex-
posing himself to humiliation.

---

5. Ibid.

Our degree of cultural knowledge—which is to say, most often, our lack of cultural knowledge—is something we guard closely, and so, too, are the lies we resort to in order to conceal our foibles. With a confidant other than a machine, Dempsey would not have risked acknowledging that he, like the rest of us, frequently talks about books he hasn't read. Such secrecy is a defense mechanism we use to hide the gaps in our learning and thus make ourselves presentable in the eyes of others—and in our own eyes as well.

Believing he is conversing with a mere machine, Dempsey reveals himself in all his naked truth to one of the people who most strongly motivate his instinct for self-protection. First of all, he reveals his true hatred for one of his colleagues, a feeling that the rules of polite society and above all of academia oblige him to disguise. But second, he reveals another truth that lurks behind academia's polite conventions about culture: that the way we approach cultural objects is often both violent and approximate.

As long as we strive for an image of cultural literacy that only serves to disguise us from others and ourselves, our more or less unconscious shame about the real nature of our interaction with books will weigh on all our relations with them and everything we say about them. If we really intend to find adequate solutions to our daily confrontations with our shortcomings, we need to recognize this shame and analyze its foundations. Only in doing so can we hope to survive the avalanche of fragments of books that threatens to engulf us, in the face of which our deepest identity is revealed to be in permanent danger.

≈

If Dempsey is disinclined to confess—except to a computer—that, like the rest of us, he sometimes talks about books he hasn't read, this is not the case for the characters in another of Lodge's novels, *Changing Places*, who stage a veritable game of truth about unread books.

The game is the invention of the same Philip Swallow whose possible appointment to the UNESCO Chair so appalled Dempsey in *Small World*. In *Changing Places*, which unfolds several years earlier, the British professor Swallow (at a humbler phase of his career) exchanges academic positions with a brilliant American professor from the West Coast, Morris Zapp. The job swap is quickly compounded by the two men swapping wives as well.

During his stay in California, Swallow initiates a few students into a game he calls Humiliation:

> He taught them a game he had invented as a postgraduate student, in which each person had to think of a well-known book he hadn't read, and scored a point for every person present who *had* read it. The Confederate Soldier and Carol were joint winners, scoring four points out of a possible five with *Steppenwolf* [6] and *The Story of O* [7] respectively, Philip in each case accounting for the odd point. His own nomination, *Oliver Twist* [8]— usually a certain winner—was nowhere. [9]

---

6. SB and FB−.
7. SB and HB++.
8. HB++.
9. *Changing Places* (London: Penguin, 1975), p. 96.

One sees why the game is called Humiliation. To score points, each person has to come up with books that nearly everyone has read, but which he hasn't. Contrary to the ordinary goals of parlor games, especially in academia, where displaying one's cultural sophistication is usually the goal, the game is based on exhibiting one's lack of cultural knowledge. It is hard to imagine a more perfect encapsulation of the way our displays of culture in social settings, before the mirror of others, awakens unreasonable feelings of shame.

The game thus consists in humiliating yourself as much as possible: the more you humiliate yourself, the more likely you are to win. But there is an additional twist, which is that victory also depends on sincerity. To win, you must not only give the name of a well-known book, but also convince the others that you have told the truth about not having read it. If you give the name of a book that is too well known, such that it is actually implausible for you not to have read it, the other players have the right to reject your statement. The chance of winning is thus proportional to the players' trust in the person confessing his ignorance, and so also in proportion to the genuineness of the player's humiliation.

Another round of Humiliation is played later on in the novel and is recounted to us by Désirée, the wife of Morris Zapp, the American professor, in a letter to her husband. Désirée has started sleeping with Swallow, the Brit having thus replaced Zapp absolutely. During a faculty gathering, Swallow proposes that they play Humiliation. However, one of the professors present, Howard Ringbaum, finds it hard to swallow the impossible situation in which players are placed, that of being able to succeed only by losing and of gaining prestige only to the extent that they humiliate themselves:

> You know Howard, he has a pathological urge to succeed and a pathological fear of being thought uncultured, and this game set his two urges at war with each other, because he could succeed in the game only by exposing a gap in his culture. At first his psyche just couldn't absorb the paradox and he named some eighteenth-century book so obscure I can't remember the name of it. Of course, he came last in the final score, and sulked.[10]

Ringbaum withdraws from the game, which is continued with such titles as Milton's *Paradise Regained*,[11] which the chairman of the English department, to the stupefaction of all present, confesses to not having read. But Ringbaum keeps an eye on what's going on and abruptly decides, at one point, to intervene:

> Well, on the third round, Sy was leading the field with *Hiawatha*,[12] Mr. Swallow being the only other person who hadn't read it, when suddenly Howard slammed his fist on the table, jutted his jaw about six feet over the table and said:
>   *"Hamlet!"*

---

10. Ibid., p. 135.
11. HB++.
12. UB−.

Well, of course, we all laughed, not very much because it didn't seem much of a joke. In fact it wasn't a joke at all. Howard admitted to having seen the Laurence Olivier movie, but insisted that he had never read the text of *Hamlet*. Nobody believed him of course, and this made him sore as hell. He said did we think he was lying and Sy more or less implied that we did. Upon which Howard flew into a great rage and insisted on swearing a solemn oath that he had never read the play. Sy apologized through tight lips for having doubted his word. By this time, of course, we were all cold sober with embarrassment. Howard left, and the rest of us stood around while trying to pretend nothing had happened.[13]

≈

The example of *Hamlet*—arguably the greatest work in the English canon, and whose symbolic import is thus significant—shows the complexity inherent in the game of truth, a complexity that is compounded in the case of academia. In point of fact, a professor of English literature runs only a minimal risk in admitting—or pretending to admit—that he hasn't read *Hamlet*. For one thing, no one is likely to believe him. And for another, the play is so well known that it is not necessary to have read it to speak about it. If it is true that he hasn't "read" *Hamlet*, Ringbaum certainly has at his

---

13. *Changing Places*, p. 136.

disposal a great deal of information about it and, in addition to Laurence Olivier's movie adaptation, is familiar with other plays by Shakespeare. Even without having had access to its contents, he is perfectly well equipped to gauge its position within the collective library.

Thus everything might have gone swimmingly if Ringbaum—as a result of the latent violence of the game, but also due to the psychological conflict mentioned by Désirée—had not committed an error, which was to not allow the *ambiguity* on the subject of his knowledge of the play to persist. In insisting on his ignorance, he excluded himself from the indefinite cultural space that we generally allow to reign between ourselves and others, within which we tacitly accord ourselves—and simultaneously accord them—a margin of ignorance. We do of course know at some level that all cultural literacy, even the most highly developed, is constructed around gaps and fissures (Lodge mentions Howard's fear of "a gap in his culture") that are no real obstacle to its taking on a certain consistency as a body of information.

This realm of communication about books—and more generally about culture—might be characterized as a *virtual library*,[14] both because it is a space dominated by images (images of oneself, in particular) rather than books and because it is not a realm based in reality. It is subject to a number of

---

14. The third type of library that I am introducing here, the *virtual library*, is the realm in which books are discussed, in either written or oral form, with other people. It is a mobile sector of every culture's *collective library* and is located at the point of intersection of the various *inner libraries* of each participant in the discussion.

rules whose goal is to maintain it as a consensual space in which books are replaced by fictions of books. It is also a realm of play, not unlike that of childhood or the theater, a kind of play that can be pursued only if the principal rules are not transgressed.

One of the implicit rules of the virtual library is that we must not attempt to find out the extent to which someone who claims he has read a book has actually done so, for two reasons. The first is that life in the virtual library would quickly become unlivable if not for a certain amount of ambiguity around the truth of our statements, and if we were instead forced to reply clearly to questions about what exactly we had read. The other reason is that the very notion of what sincerity would mean is questionable, since knowing what is meant by *having read a book*, as we have seen, is highly problematic.

In declaring that he hasn't "read" *Hamlet*, in telling the truth—or what he believes to be the truth—Ringbaum violates the fundamental rule of the virtual library, which is that it is fine to talk about books one hasn't read. In so doing, he transforms the space of this exchange, through a brutal exposure of his private sphere, into a place of violence. Through this gesture, indeed, he unveils the truth of culture, which is that it is a theater charged with concealing individual ignorance and the fragmentation of knowledge. In so doing, he does not merely expose his nakedness but effects a kind of psychic rape of the others.

The violence of the reaction to which he will be subjected is commensurate with the violence he has exercised on the normally playful stage of the virtual library. In daring to utter the truth about his reading of Shakespeare, but also, as a consequence, about the nature of the space in which we talk about books, Ringbaum finds himself exiled from it. His sanction is not long in coming, as recounted by Désirée at the end of her letter:

> A piquant incident, you must admit—but wait till I tell you the sequel. Howard Ringbaum unexpectedly flunked his review three days later and it's generally supposed that this was because the English Department dared not give tenure to a man who publicly admitted to not having read *Hamlet*. The story had been buzzed all round the campus, of course, and there was even a paragraph alluding to it in the *Euphoric State Daily*. Furthermore, as this created an unexpected vacancy in the Department, they've reconsidered the case of Kroop and offered him tenure after all. I don't suppose he's read *Hamlet* either, but nobody was asking.[15]

As Désirée observes, the question of whether the person replacing Ringbaum—who at this point has no other choice than to kill himself—has read *Hamlet* is secondary. What is important is that he not step out of the intermediary space of virtual books, which allows us to live and communicate with others. And rather than risk any violence to that consensual space, which cloaks us like a protective garment, we may well prefer to avoid asking a candidate, at least in this context, the exact extent of his knowledge of Shakespeare.

---

15. *Changing Places*, p. 136.

∾

Through the analysis of this virtual space and its protective function, we see clearly that it is not just shame, linked to scenarios from childhood, that is in the offing when we dare to speak about books we haven't read, but a more serious threat to our self-image and the image we convey to others. In the intellectual circles where writing still counts, the books we have read form an integral part of our image, and we call that image into question when we venture to publicly announce our inner library's limits.

In this cultural context, books—whether read or unread—form a kind of second language to which we can turn to talk about ourselves, to communicate with others, and to defend ourselves in conflict. Like language, books serve to express us, but also to complete us, furnishing, through a variety of excerpted and reworked fragments, the missing elements of our personality.

Like words, books, in representing us, also deform what we are. We cannot coincide completely with the image the totality of our reading presents; whether the image makes us look better or worse than we should, behind it all our particularities vanish. And especially since books are often present within us only as little-known or forgotten fragments, we are often out of phase with the books that are our public face; they are as inadequate in the end as any other language.

In talking about books, we find ourselves exchanging not so much cultural objects as the very parts of ourselves we need to shore up our coherence during these threats to our narcissistic selves. Our feelings of shame arise because our very identity is imperiled by these exchanges, whence the imperative that the virtual space in which we stage them remain marked by ambiguity and play.

In this regard, this ambiguous social space is the opposite of school—a realm of violence driven by the fantasy that there exists such a thing as thorough reading, and a place where everything is calibrated to determine whether the students have truly read the books about which they speak and face interrogation. Such an aim is, in the end, illusory, for reading does not obey the hard logic of true and false, of waving off ambiguity and evaluating with certitude whether readers are telling the truth.

When Ringbaum insists on transforming that realm of play in which books are discussed, that space of constant negotiation and intermittent hypocrisy, into a realm of truth, he locks himself into a paradox that will lead him into madness. Unable to tolerate the indecisiveness of the space within which the discussion about books takes place, he insists on seeing himself reflected in the other players' eyes as the best—which, given the particularity of Swallow's game, is to say the worst. He succeeds, on his own terms, in assuming this image that is less unsettling to him, because it is less ambiguous; but in the end it leads him, reconciled with himself though he may be, to his ruin.

∾

To speak without shame about books we haven't read, we would thus do well to free ourselves of the oppressive image of cultural literacy without gaps, as transmitted and imposed by family and school, for we can strive toward this image for a lifetime without ever managing to coincide with it. Truth destined for others is less important than truthfulness to ourselves, something attainable only by those who free themselves from the obligation to seem cultivated, which tyrannizes us from within and prevents us from being ourselves.

Imposing Your Ideas

(in which Balzac proves that one key to imposing
your point of view on a book is to remember
that the book is not a fixed object, and that
even tying it up with string will not be
sufficient to stop its motion)

As LONG AS you have the courage, therefore, there is no reason not to say frankly that you haven't read any particular
book, nor to abstain from expressing your thoughts about it.
The experience of not having read a book is the most common of scenarios, and only in accepting our non-reading
without shame can we begin to take an interest in what is actually at stake, which is not a book but a complex interpersonal
situation of which the book is less the object than the consequence.

Books are not insensitive to what is said around them, in
fact, but may be changed by it in just the time it takes us to
have a conversation. This mobility of the text is the second
great uncertainty of the ambiguous realm that is the virtual
library. It compounds the kind of uncertainty we have just

examined—our uncertainty about how well those who talk about books actually know them—and will be crucial to our delineation of what strategies to adopt in these situations. These strategies will be all the more relevant in that they will not depend on an image of books as fixed objects, but instead assume that the participants in a fast-moving discussion, especially if they have the strength to impose their own points of view, can change the text itself.

∾

Lucien Chardon, the hero of Balzac's novel *Lost Illusions*,[1] is the son of an apothecary from Angoulême who dreams of retrieving the aristocratic name of his mother, who was born de Rubempré. Having fallen in love with a woman of the local nobility, Madame de Bargeton, he follows her to Paris, leaving behind his best friend, the printer David Séchard, who has married Lucien's sister Eve. But he is also heading for the capital with an eye to making his name in the world of letters, and he brings with him his first texts, a collection of poems called *Les Marguerites*[2] and a historical novel called *L'Archer de Charles IX.*[3]

In Paris, Lucien finds his way into the small circle of intellectuals in control of publishing and the press and quickly discovers the reality—far removed from his illusions—of the milieu in which literature and art are produced. Its true nature

---

1. SB, HB, and FB+.
2. UB−−.
3. UB+.

is brutally revealed to him in a conversation with one of his new friends, a journalist named Étienne Lousteau. Lousteau, short of money, is forced to resell several books to a bookseller named Barbet. The pages of several of them turn out to have not even been cut, even though Lousteau has promised reviews of them to the editor of a newspaper:

> Barbet looked over the books, carefully examining the edges and the covers.
>
> "Oh! They're in perfect condition!" exclaimed Lousteau. "The leaves of *Travels in Egypt*[4] aren't cut, nor the Paul de Kock, nor the Ducange, nor the one on the mantelpiece, *Reflections on Symbolism*.[5] I'll throw that one in, the mythology in it is so boring. I'll give it to you so that I needn't watch thousands of mites swarming out of it."
>
> "But," asked Lucien, "how will you write your reviews on them?"
>
> Barbet gave Lucien a glance of profound astonishment and then looked back at Lousteau with a snigger. "It's plain to see that this gentleman hasn't the misfortune to be a man of letters."[6]

Surprised that one might devote an article to a book one hasn't read, Lucien cannot resist asking Lousteau how he plans to honor his promise to the newspaper editor:

---

4. UB–.
5. UB– –.
6. Balzac, *Lost Illusions*, translated by Herbert J. Hunt (London: Penguin Books, 1971), p. 255.

"But what about your review article?" asked Lucien as they drove away to the Palais-Royal.

"Pooh! You've no idea how they're dashed off. Take *Travels in Egypt*: I opened the book and read a bit here and there without cutting the pages, and I discovered eleven mistakes in the French. I shall write a column to the effect that even if the author can interpret the duck-lingo carved on the Egyptian pebbles they call obelisks, he doesn't know his own language—and I shall prove it to him. I shall say that instead of talking about natural history and antiquities he ought only to have concerned himself with the future of Egypt, the progress of civilization, the means of winning Egypt over to France, which, after conquering it and then losing it again, could still establish a moral ascendancy over it. Then a few pages of patriotic twaddle, the whole interlarded with tirades on Marseilles, the Levant and our trading interests."[7]

When Lucien asks what Lousteau would have done if the author *had* discussed politics, his friend replies without missing a beat that he would have reproached the writer for boring his reader with political talk, rather than concerning himself with Art by focusing on the picturesque aspects of the country. In any event, he relies in the end on another method: he gets his girlfriend, Florine, an actress and "the greatest reader of novels in the world," to read the book.

---

7. Ibid., p. 258.

Only when she declares herself bored by what she calls "author's sentences" does he start to take the book seriously and ask the bookseller for a new copy so that he can write a favorable article.

~

Here we encounter once again some of the varieties of non-reading that we have already identified, in which we either surmise what a book is about without knowing it at all; skim through it; or base our opinions on the opinions of others. Lucien, nonetheless, is a bit surprised by his friend's critical method and confesses his astonishment to him:

> "Great Heavens! But what about criticism, the sacred task of criticism?" said Lucien, still imbued with the doctrines of the Cénacle.
>
> "My dear chap," said Lousteau. "Criticism's a scrubbing-brush which you mustn't use on flimsy materials—it would tear them to shreds. Now listen, let's stop talking shop. You see this mark?" he asked, pointing to the manuscript of *Les Marguerites*. "I've inked a line in between the string and the paper. If Dauriat reads your manuscript, he certainly won't be able to put the string back along the line. So your manuscript is as good as sealed. It's not a bad dodge for the experiment you want to make. One more thing, just remember that you won't get into that sweatshop by yourself and without a sponsor: you'd be like those

young hopefuls who go round to ten publishers before
they find one who'll even offer them a chair . . ."[8]

Thus does Lousteau pitilessly pursue the task of disillu-
sioning his friend, advising him, before Lucien submits his
poetry manuscript to one of the most important publishers
in Paris, to devise a test—a piece of ink-stained string that
binds the book shut—of not only whether Dauriat has read
it, but whether he has even opened it.

When Lucien returns to see Dauriat and asks whether he's
read the poems, Dauriat gives him hardly any hope of being
published:

"Indeed I have," said Dauriat, leaning forward in his arm-
chair like an oriental potentate. "I've glanced through the
collection of poems and got a man of taste, a good judge,
to read them, for I don't claim to be a connoisseur in poetry. I, my friend, buy ready-made reputations as an En-
glishman buys ready-made love. You are as great a poet,
my boy, as you are a handsome youngster. On my word as
an honest man—I don't mean as a publisher, mind you—
your sonnets are magnificent and you've put good work
into them, a rare enough thing when one has inspiration
and verve. In short, you know how to rhyme—one of
the qualities of the modern school. Your *Marguerites*
make a fine book, but there's no money in them, and I
can only go in for very big undertakings."[9]

---

8. Ibid., p. 259.
9. Ibid., p. 353.

While he rejects the manuscript and does not claim to have read it all the way through, Dauriat nevertheless maintains that he has gained some acquaintance with the book; he is even able to make a few stylistic remarks, on the quality of the rhymes, for example. But Lousteau's precaution of sealing the manuscript enables the two friends to take a closer look:

"Have you the manuscript with you?" asked Lucien, coldly.

"Here it is, my friend," repled Dauriat, who was now adopting singularly sugary tones with Lucien.

Lucien took the scroll without looking to see the position of the string, so certain it seemed that Dauriat had read the *Marguerites*. He went out with Lousteau without appearing either dismayed or discontented. Dauriat walked through the shop with the two friends talking about his newspaper and that of Lousteau. Lucien was unconcernedly toying with the manuscript of the *Marguerites*.

"Do you believe Dauriat read your sonnets or had them read?" Étienne whispered to Lucien.

"Yes," said Lucien.

"Look at the 'seals'!"

Lucien perceived that the ink-lines and the string were in a state of perfect conjunction.[10]

Despite not having opened the manuscript, Dauriat has no trouble elaborating on his initial opinion of the anthology and providing further details:

---

10. Ibid., p. 355.

"Which sonnet did you most particularly notice?" Lucien asked the publisher, turning pale with suppressed rage.

"They are all worthy of notice, my friend," Dauriat replied. "But the one on the marguerite is delicious and ends with a very subtle and delicate thought. By that I divined what success your prose is bound to obtain."[11]

∼

That it is not necessary to read a book to speak about it is illustrated a second time as Lucien and Lousteau continue their dialogue. Lousteau proposes to his friend that as revenge against the publisher's insult, Lucien should write an incendiary article attacking a book by the writer Nathan, an author championed by Dauriat. But the quality of the book is so patently apparent that Lucien has no idea how to begin criticizing it. Laughing, Lousteau explains that it is time for Lucien to learn his trade, and with it the acrobatic ability to change the beauties of a book into defects—that is, to transform a masterpiece into an "insipid bit of stupidity."[12]

Lousteau then shows him how to denigrate a book that one holds in the highest regard. His method is to make an opening statement in which one tells the "truth" and praises the book. The public, pleased by this positive beginning and inclined to be trusting, will judge the critic to be impartial and prepare to follow his lead.

---

11. Ibid.
12. Ibid., p. 357.

At this juncture, Lousteau endeavors to show that Nathan's work is characteristic of a trend within which French literature has become trapped. This literary trend is characterized by an overreliance on description and dialogue—an excess of images, in other words—at the expense of thought, which has historically dominated the great works of French literature. To be sure, Lousteau argues, Walter Scott is remarkable, but "there's room only for truly original minds," and his influence on his successors has been deleterious.[13]

This opposition between a "literature of ideas" and a "literature of images" is then turned against Nathan, who is but an imitator and has only the outward trappings of talent. If his work is deserving, it is also dangerous, since it opens literature up to the mob by spurring a multitude of minor authors to imitate this facile form. As a counterpoint to this decadence, Lousteau suggests, Lucien should invoke the struggle of those writers resisting the romantic invasion and continuing in the footsteps of Voltaire by defending ideas against images.

And by no means is this the only method in Lousteau's arsenal for dispatching a book. He demonstrates to Lucien other solutions as well, such as the "leading article" that entails "smothering the book between two promises."[14] According to this strategy, the article starts off by announcing a commentary on the book, then loses itself in general considerations that necessitate postponing the real critique to a subsequent article, which will never appear.

---

13. Ibid.
14. Ibid., p. 358.

~

The example of Nathan's book would seem to be a departure from the previous ones we have studied, since Lucien is trying to discuss a book that he has in fact read. But the principle behind Lousteau's strategy here is the same one that applies to Lucien's unread poems or to *Travels in Egypt*: that the content of a book has little bearing on the commentary the book deserves. In this example from Balzac, it even becomes possible, in a kind of final paradox or hunger for provocation, to begin reading it.

In all three cases in Balzac—for *Travels in Egypt*, as well as for the books by Lucien or Nathan—the commentary is not related to the book, but to the author. It is the author's value, his place in the literary system, that determines the value of the book. As Lousteau says explicitly to Lucien, it may at times even be just the publisher who is implicated: "What you're writing here isn't an article against Nathan, but one against Dauriat: that calls for a pickaxe. A pickaxe glances off a fine work, but it cuts right through to a bad one: in the first case, it hurts only the publisher; in the second case, it does the public a service."[15]

An author's place in the literary system is eminently malleable, moreover, which means that the value of a book is malleable as well. Lucien soon sees this for himself, for as soon as Dauriat reads his article on Nathan's book, any difficulty about publishing Lucien's book of poems vanishes.

---

15. Ibid., p. 359.

The bookseller even travels to his home to sign their peace agreement:

> He pulled out an elegant pocket-book, drew three thousand-franc notes from it, put them on a plate and offered them to Lucien with the obsequiousness of a courtesan and said: "Does that satisfy you, Monsieur?"
>
> "Yes," said the poet. A wave of bliss hitherto unexperienced swept over him at the sight of this unexpected sum. He held himself in, but he wanted to sing, to leap up and down. He believed in the existence of wizards and Aladdin's wonderful lamp; in short he believed he had a genius at his command.
>
> "So the *Marguerites* will belong to me?" asked the publisher. "But you'll never attack any of my publications?"
>
> "The *Marguerites* are yours, but I can't pledge my pen. It belongs to my friends, just as theirs belongs to me."
>
> "But after all, you are becoming one of my authors. All my authors are my friends. You'll do no damage to my affairs without my being warned of any attacks so that I can forestall them?"
>
> "Agreed."
>
> "Here's to your future fame!" said Dauriat, raising his glass.
>
> "Obviously you've read the *Marguerites*," said Lucien.[16]

---

16. Ibid., p. 366.

Dauriat is not at all affected by the allusion to his non-reading of *Les Marguerites*. His judgment of it has changed simply because the author of the work has changed:

"My boy, buying the *Marguerites* without knowing them is the finest flattery a publisher can permit himself. In six months you'll be a great poet; articles will be written about you. People are afraid of you, so I need do nothing to get your book sold. I'm the same business man today as I was four days ago. It's not I who have changed, it's you. Last week I wouldn't have given a fig leaf for your sonnets, but your position today turns them into something rich and rare."

"Oh well," said Lucien, being now in a mocking and charmingly provocative frame of mind since he felt all the pleasures of a sultan in possessing a beautiful mistress and in being assured of success. "Even if you haven't read my sonnets, you've read my article."

"Yes, my friend. Otherwise should I have come along so promptly? Unfortunately, it's very fine, this terrible article."[17]

Lucien has further disillusionments yet in store. The very evening his article is published, Lousteau explains to him that he has just met Nathan, who is desperate, and that it is too dangerous to have him as one's enemy. He thus advises Lucien

17. Ibid., p. 367.

to "squirt showers of praise in his face."[18] Lucien is astonished that he is now being asked for a positive article about a book he has just criticized, while his friends once again find his naïveté hilarious. At this point, he learns that one of them had taken the precaution of going by the newspaper offices and changing the signature on his article to a minimally compromising letter *C*. Thus there is nothing to prevent Lucien from writing another article for a different newspaper, and signing this time with the letter *L*.

But Lucien can't think of anything to add to his original opinion. It thus falls to Blondet, another of his friends, to demonstrate the reverse of the argument that Lousteau had previously offered, and to explain to Lucien that "every idea has its front side and its reverse side, and no one can presume to state which side is which. Everything is bilateral in the domain of thought. Ideas are two-sided. Janus is the tutelary deity of criticism and the symbol of genius."[19] Blondet thus suggests that in this second article, Lucien should attack the fashionable theory positing the existence of one literature of ideas and another literature of images, whereas clearly the most refined literary art assumes the obligation of combining the two.

As a final touch, Blondet even proposes to Lucien that he not limit himself to two articles signed "C." and "L." but compose a third, this time signed "de Rubempré," which would reconcile the two others by demonstrating that the

18. Ibid., p. 372.
19. Ibid., p. 372.

breadth of the debates about Nathan's book are a sure sign of its importance.

∾

These scenes from Balzac magnify the features of what I have called the virtual library to the point of caricature. In the intellectual milieu that Balzac describes, the only thing that matters is the social positions of the actors. Treated as mere shadows of their authors, the books themselves make no intervention, and nor does anyone make the effort to read them before issuing a judgment, whether as critic or publisher. Indeed, the books themselves are not at stake; they have been replaced by other intermediary objects that have no content in themselves, and which are defined solely by the unstable social and psychological forces that bombard them.

As in Lodge's game, shame remains an essential component in the organization of the virtual library, but in this case its function is ironically reversed. Humiliation no longer threatens the individual who hasn't read a book, but the one who has; reading is seen as a degrading task that may be left to a woman of the demimonde. But this space still remains organized around the feeling of shame, and the resulting world, beyond its apparent playfulness, is remarkably psychically violent.

In Balzac as in Lodge, the game is played for positions of power. The importance of power in the reception of texts is easy to perceive in *Lost Illusions*, for it is directly and immediately connected to a book's literary value. A favorable review contributes to power, while inversely, power guarantees favorable reviews. It can even serve to confirm, as in Lucien's case, the quality of the text.

In a way, the universe described by Balzac is the reverse of Lodge's. Whereas the world of the British academic is characterized by the taboo of non-reading (so much so that the character who dares to flaunt it is promptly excluded from the cultural space), the transgression of the taboo is so generalized in Balzac that non-reading becomes the rule, and a kind of taboo ends up being placed on reading, which is considered humiliating.

Two forms of transgression are pervasive in this world. First, it is permitted, and even recommended, that critics should speak about books without opening them, and Lucien is subjected to ridicule when he suggests that the situation could proceed otherwise. The transgression of non-reading is such a commonplace here that in the end it is no longer a transgression; no one even thinks of reading a book anymore. Only when a person unacquainted with journalistic behavior enters the world of letters do its habitués momentarily evoke the possibility of reading—and then only to reject it immediately.

This first transgression, that of universal non-reading, is compounded by a second one, which insists that any opinion you sustain about a book is equally valid. In a world where opening a book in order to talk about it is laughable, any opinion is fine as long as you can defend it. The book itself, reduced to pure pretext, has, in a sense, ceased to exist.

≈

This double transgression of the conventional rules of talking about books is a sign of a perverse society wherein all books, and all the endlessly reversible judgments of books, end up being the equivalent of any others. But the position held by Lucien's friends in this case, even if it resembles sophistry, nevertheless reveals certain truths about reading and the way we talk about books.

Lousteau and Blondet's attitude in encouraging Lucien to write contradictory articles would be shocking if the two articles were about exactly the same book. What Balzac is suggesting is that it is not exactly the same in the two cases. To be sure, the physical book remains identical to itself, but no longer represents the same knot of relationships once Nathan's position in society evolves. Similarly, once Lucien has attained a certain social position, his *Marguerites* becomes a rather different collection of poems.

In each case, the book does not change materially, but it undergoes modifications to its situation in the collective library. What Balzac is calling our attention to is the importance of context. He caricatures this importance, certainly, but his portrait has the merit all the same of showing how determining it can be. To allow context to become part of the equation means remembering that a book is not fixed once and for all but is a moving object, and that its mobility is in part a function of the set of power relations woven around it.

If the author changes and the book changes as well, can it at least be said that we are always dealing with the same reader? Nothing is less clear, judging by the speed with which Lucien alters his opinion of Nathan's book after his talk with Lousteau:

Lucien was stupefied as he listened to Lousteau's words: the scales fell from his eyes and he became alive to literary truths of which he had not even guessed.

"But what you tell me," he exclaimed, "is full of reason and relevance."

"If it were not, how could you make an attack on Nathan's book?" said Lousteau.[20]

A brief conversation with Lousteau is thus sufficient for Lucien to form a different opinion about Nathan's book, and that without even looking at it anew. It is not the book as such that is in play, therefore (since Lucien cannot know what he would feel if he were to reread it), but the interplay of comments about it in society. That new opinion becomes so much his own that he can no longer modify it, and when Lousteau proposes to him that he ought to write a second, favorable article, he tries to recuse himself, claiming that he is now incapable of writing a single word of praise. His friends, however, intervene to unsettle him once more and give him fresh access to his initial sentiment:

Next morning, it turned out that the previous day's ideas had germinated, as happens with all minds which are bursting with sap and whose faculties have as yet had little exercise. Lucien derived pleasure from thinking out this new article and set about it with enthusiasm. From his pen flowed all the fine sallies born of paradox.

---

20. Ibid., p. 358.

He was witty and mocking, he even rose to new reflex-
ions on feeling, ideas, and imagery in literature. With
subtle ingenuity, in order to praise Nathan, he captured
the first impressions about the book . . . [21]

We may thus wonder whether Lucien is anxious less about
the mobility of the book than about his own inner mobility
and what he is little by little discovering about it. He can assume the different intellectual and psychic positions that
Blondet proposes to him without any harm, successively and
even simultaneously. It is less his friends' contempt for books
that is unsettling than his own unfaithfulness both to others
and to himself, an unfaithfulness that will, in the end, lead to
his downfall.[22]

∽

The acknowledgment that books are mobile objects rather
than fixed texts is indeed destabilizing, since it reflects back
our own uncertainty—which is to say, our folly. In facing that
confrontation more forthrightly than Lucien, however, we
may be able to simultaneously approach works in their richness and reduce the awkwardness of our discussions about
them.

Indeed, to acknowledge both the mobility of a text and
our own mobility is a major advantage, one that confers great

---

21. Ibid., p. 377.
22. Having first rallied to the liberals, Lucien later attempts a rapprochement
with the monarchists, and he finally ends up with everyone against him.

freedom to impose our judgments of books on others. Balzac's heroes demonstrate the remarkable plasticity of the virtual library and the ease with which it can be bent to the requirements of anyone who—having read a book or not—is determined to persevere through the remarks of so-called readers to assert the truth of his perceptions.

Inventing Books

(in which, reading Sōseki, we follow the advice of
a cat and an artist in gold-rimmed spectacles, who
each, in different fields of activity, proclaim
the necessity of invention)

IF A BOOK is less a book than it is the whole of the discussion
about it, we must pay attention to that discussion in order to
talk about the book without reading it. For it is not the book
itself that is at stake, but what it has become within the critical space in which it intervenes and is continually transformed. It is this moving object, a supple fabric of relations
between texts and beings, about which one must be in a position to formulate accurate statements at the right moment.

The constant modification of books affects not only their
value (we have seen in the example from Balzac how quickly
this may shift along with the place of the author in literary
politics), but also their *content*, which is no more stable, and
which undergoes palpable variation as a result of the things
said about it. This mobility of the text should not be understood as a drawback. To the contrary, for someone prepared to

turn it to his advantage, it offers a remarkable opportunity to become the creator of the books he hasn't read.

~

In the novel *I Am a Cat*,[1] perhaps his best-known work, the Japanese writer Natsume Sōseki entrusts the narration of his tale to a cat, who begins his autobiography with these words:

> I am a cat but as yet I have no name.
>
> I haven't the faintest idea of where I was born. The first thing I do remember is that I was crying "meow, meow," somewhere in a gloomy damp place. It was there that I met a human being for the first time in my life. Though I found this all out at a later date, I learned that this human being was called a Student, one of the most ferocious of the human race.[2]

The novel's feline narrator, who will remain anonymous throughout the work, has little luck in this first encounter with the human species. He encounters a student who mistreats him, and he wakes up delirious and far from home. He then slips inside an unknown house, where he is fortunate enough to be welcomed by the owner, a professor. *I Am a Cat* is devoted to recounting his life in that house, where he takes up residence.

---

1. SB++.
2. *I Am a Cat*, translated by Katsue Shibata and Motonari Kai (Tokyo: Kenkyusha, 1961), p. 1.

Although the point of view of our cat narrator—the feline point of view—is dominant in the book, the reader is granted a relatively complex perspective of his world. The narrator, in fact, is not an uncultivated animal, but a cat endowed with a number of skills, such as the ability to follow a conversation and even to read.

But the cat does not forget his origins; he remains connected to the feline world. He thus enters into protracted relations with two cats from his new neighborhood, the female cat Mike and the male cat Kuro. Kuro is the reigning master of the area, forcing others to respect him through physical strength. But he also occupies a special position in the novel as the animal emblem of a whole series of characters whose common characteristic is boastfulness. Kuro's bragging centers on various domains important to cats, such as the number of mice caught, an area in which he shows no qualms about exaggerating his prowess.

∾

Kuro has a counterpart among the humans who frequent the professor's house. The narrator cat refers to that individual, M., as "the artist in gold-rimmed spectacles," and he has the peculiar habit of recounting whatever stories come into his head, for the sheer pleasure of leading his listener astray.

At the beginning of the book, seeing that the professor is interested in painting and would like to do some himself, M. tells him about the Italian painter Andrea del Sarto and shares with him the theory that del Sarto would have recommended painting as much as possible in imitation of nature and learning first of all how to sketch. The professor puts his trust in this advice, but fails to become a painter. The artist then reveals to him that he has in fact invented all the alleged remarks of Andrea del Sarto and that he often takes pleasure in making up stories and playing on people's credulity:

> The artist was greatly enjoying himself. Listening to all this from the veranda, I couldn't help wondering what my master would write in his diary about that conversation. The artist was a person who took great pleasure in fooling others. As if he did not realize how his joke about Andrea del Sarto hurt my master, he boasted more: "When playing jokes, some people take them so seriously that they reveal great comic beauty, and it's a lot of fun. The other day I told a student that Nicholas Nickleby had advised Gibbon to translate his great *History of the French Revolution*[3] from a French textbook and to have it published under his own name. This student has an extremely good memory and made a speech at the Japanese Literary Circle quoting everything I had told him. There were about a hundred people in the audience and they all listened very attentively."[4]

The Nickleby story is absurd on two levels. For one thing, it would be more than a little difficult for the fictional character Nicholas Nickleby to give advice to Edward Gibbon,

---

3. UB–.
4. Sōseki, op. cit., pp. 13–14.

an entirely real British historian. Second, even if the two men did belong to the same universe, they would still not have been able to enter into dialogue, since Nickleby appeared for the first time in the world of letters in 1838, by which date Gibbon had already been dead for nearly fifty years.

If, in this first example, the artist makes up stories without compunction, the situation is slightly different in the next one he gives, which directly concerns our consideration of unread books:

> "Then there's another time. One evening, at a gather-ing of writers, the conversation turned to Harrison's his-torical novel *Theophano*.[5] I said that it was one of the best historical novels ever written, especially the part where the heroine dies. 'That really gives you the creeps'— that's what I said. An author who was sitting opposite me was one of those types who cannot and will not say no to anything. He immediately voiced the opinion that that was a most famous passage. I knew right away that he had never read any more of the story than I had."[6]

This kind of cynicism raises several questions, one of which the professor asks the artist immediately:

> With wide eyes, my nervous and weak-stomached master asked, "What would you have done if the other man had really read the story?"

---

5. SB–.
6. Sōseki, op. cit., p. 14.

The artist did not show any excitement. He thought nothing of fooling other people. The only thing that counted was not to be caught in the act.

"All I would have to do is to say that I had made a mistake in the title or something to that effect." He kept on laughing.[7]

If you have begun talking about a book imprudently and your remarks are challenged, nothing prevents you from backtracking and declaring that you've made a mistake. Our *unreading* or forgetting plays such a significant role that there is little risk in declaring yourself the victim of one of the many lapses in memory induced by our reading— and non-reading—of books. Even a book that we recall with great precision is in some sense a screen book, behind which our own inner book is concealed. But in this particular case, is it really the best solution for the artist to admit his error?

~

In fact, Sōseki's text raises an interesting problem of logic. The artist with gold-rimmed spectacles invents a scene about the death of the heroine, so when, instead of challenging the existence of such a scene in Harrison's book, the other man says approvingly that it is splendid indeed, he is presumed to be revealed as a liar as well. But how can the artist know for

---

7. Ibid.

sure that he is dealing with a non-reader if he himself has never read the novel?

In the situation described by Sōseki, where two non-readers of the same book carry on a dialogue about it, it is actually impossible for either of the non-readers to know whether the other is lying. There can be no conviction that anyone is lying in a conversation about a book without at least one of the participants knowing the book or having at least a vague idea of it.

But is the situation different when one of the two conversationalists, or both, have "read" the book? Sōseki's anecdote, like the game of truth in Lodge, has the merit of reminding us of the first of the two uncertainties of the virtual library, which concerns the competence of readers. It is difficult, if not impossible, to know the extent to which the person with whom you are speaking about a book is lying about having read it. Not only because there is hardly another domain in which such pronounced hypocrisy holds sway, but above all because each speaker cannot possibly know the other person's history with the book and they are thus deluding themselves if they think they can answer the question.

Such a conversation amounts to a game of dupes, in which the participants fool themselves even before fooling others, and in which their memories of books will be marked by the stakes of the situation at hand. It would, after all, be a misunderstanding of the act of reading to try to separate those who have read a certain book and those who are ignorant of it into two camps, as Lodge's professor foolishly tried to do. It is a misunderstanding both by so-called readers, who disregard the erasure and loss that accompanies every act of reading,

and so-called non-readers, who ignore the creative impulse
that can arise from every encounter with a book.

To liberate ourselves from the idea that the Other knows
whether we're lying—the Other being just as much
ourselves—is thus one of the primary conditions for being
able to talk about books with grace, whether we've read them
or not. In truth, of course, the knowledge at stake in our
comments on books is intrinsically uncertain. And the Other,
meanwhile, is a disapproving image of ourselves that we project onto our listeners, an image we have internalized based
on a culture so exhaustive, and whose importance is so firmly
drummed into us in school, that it impedes us from living and
thinking.

But our anxiety in the face of the Other's knowledge is an
obstacle to all genuine creativity about books. The idea that
the Other has read everything, and thus is better informed
than us, reduces creativity to a mere stopgap that non-readers
might resort to in a pinch. In truth, readers and non-readers
alike are caught up in an endless process of inventing books,
whether they like it or not, and the real question is not how
to escape that process, but how to increase its dynamism and
its range.

≈

This initial uncertainty about the competence of the people
we're speaking to is compounded by another kind of uncertainty, already observed in Balzac, but here emphasized such
that it bears on the book itself. If it is difficult to ascertain
what the other person knows and what we know ourselves,

this is true in part because it is not that easy to know what is in a text. This doubt not only concerns its value, as in Balzac, but extends to its so-called content as well.

Such is the case for Frederic Harrison's novel *Theophano*,[8] about which, according to the artist with gold-rimmed spectacles, one might theoretically be wrong or mislead someone else. Published in 1904, it belongs to the literary genre that might be called the Byzantine novel. It begins in AD 956 and continues to 969, and it tells of the victorious counteroffensive against Islam led by the emperor of Constantinople, Nicephorus Phocas.

The question then arises of whether the artist is making up stories by commenting on the dramatic death of the heroine (which is, moreover, another way of wondering whether Sōseki is talking about a book he hasn't read). Can one say that the heroine dies, and if the answer is yes, might her death be sufficiently moving to send chills down one's spine?

This question is not so simple to answer. The historical character one would tend to regard as the heroine— Theophano, the wife of Emperor Nicephorus, whom she helps to assassinate—does not die, but on the last page of the novel, she is imprisoned and exiled.[9] We are thus dealing with a kind of death, or at least a disappearance. A reader who *had* read the book might in good faith forget the precise circumstances of her elimination and simply remember that a

---

8. Frederic Harrison, *Theophano: The Crusade of the Tenth Century* (New York: Harper & Bros., 1904).
9. Ibid., p. 337.

misfortune befalls her, without it being possible to say that he hadn't read the book.

The problem is further complicated by the observation that there is not one heroine, but two, in the novel. The second is Princess Agatha, a discreet and admirable heroine who withdraws to a convent upon learning of the death in combat of her beloved, the emperor's companion Basil Digenes. The passage about this incident refrains from lyrical excess and is all the more successful for doing so. Thus there is a quite moving case of the disappearance of a female character, and an alleged reader's recollection that she had died would hardly seem like grounds for an evaluation of whether he had really read the book.

At an entirely different level than the factual question of whether the heroine dies, the artist is perfectly justified in praising the quality of the passage describing such an event, since in a certain sense it feels right to him, at least as an unrealized possibility. Few adventure novels of this period do not include a female character, and it is hard to see how the reader's interest might be sustained for any great length of time without including a love story. And how, in that case, would one not have the heroine die, unless one were telling a story with a happy ending, which literature is rarely inclined to do?[10]

It is thus doubly difficult to know whether the artist has read *Theophano*. In the first place, it is not that far off to say that the book features the death of a heroine, even if the word

---

10. There is no end to the number of books in world literature in which the "death of the heroine" is one of the most beautiful passages.

disappearance might be more appropriate. Moreover, being wrong on this point in no way proves that he hasn't read it. This cultural fantasy of the heroine's death is so potent that it is unsurprising that he would associate it with the book once his reading is complete, even to the point where it becomes an integral part of the book for him.

The books we talk about, in other words, are not just the actual books that would be uncovered in a complete and objective reading of the human library, but also *phantom books* that surface where the unrealized possibilities of each book meet our unconscious. These phantom books fuel our daydreams and conversations, far more than the real objects that are theoretically their source.[11]

∾

One sees how directly the discussion of a book leads us to a point where the notions of true and false, contrary to what the artist with gold-rimmed spectacles believes, lose much of their validity. It is first difficult to know whether we ourselves have read a book, so evanescent is our reading. Second, it is more or less impossible to know whether others have read it, since this would first entail their knowing such a thing.

---

11. The third type of book I am introducing here, the *phantom book*, is that mobile and ungraspable object that we call into being, in writing or in speech, when we talk about a book. It is located at the point where readers' various *screen books* meet—screen books that readers have constructed based on their *inner books*. The phantom book belongs to the virtual library of our exchanges, as the screen book belongs to the collective library and the inner book belongs to the inner library.

Finally, the content of a text is so fluid that it is difficult to assert with certainty that something is not found in it.

The virtual space of discussion about books is thus characterized by extraordinary uncertainty, which applies to the participants, incapable of stating rigorously what they have read, as much as to the moving target of their discussion. But this uncertainty is not entirely disadvantageous; it can also provide the opportunity, if those in the conversation seize the moment, to transform the virtual library into an authentic realm of fiction.

Fiction, here, should not be understood pejoratively. What I mean to say is that if its rules are respected by the occupants, the virtual library is in a position to advance an original kind of creativity. Such creativity can arise from the resonances that a book calls up in those who haven't read it. It can be individual or collective. Its aim is to construct a book more propitious to the situation in which the non-readers find themselves—a book that may have only feeble links to the original (which would be what, exactly?), but one that is as close as possible to the hypothetical meeting point of various inner books.

In another of his books, *Grass on the Wayside*,[12] Sōseki depicts a painter who has retreated to the mountains to produce a summation of his art. One day his landlady's daughter comes into his room and, seeing him with a book, asks him what he is reading. The painter answers that he doesn't know, since his practice is to open the book at random and read the

---

12. SB++.

page before his eyes without knowing anything of the rest of
the book. Reacting to the young woman's surprise, the painter
explains to her that it is more interesting for him to proceed
in this manner: "I open the book at random as though it were
a game of chance, and I read the page that ends up in front of
me, and that's what is interesting."[13]

The woman suggests that he show her his method, which
he agrees to do, eventually translating a passage from the English book in his hand into Japanese for her. The subject is
a man and a woman of whom nothing is known other than
that they are in a boat in Venice. When the young woman
asks who these characters are, the painter replies that he hasn't
the slightest idea, since he hasn't read the book and insists on
not finding out any more:

> "Who are that man and that woman?"
> "I have no idea. But that's precisely why it's interest-
> ing. We have no need to be concerned with their rela-
> tions until then. Just like you and I finding ourselves
> together, it's only the present moment that counts."[14]

What is important in the book is external to it, since it is
only a pretext or vehicle for this moment of discussion: talking about a book is less about the book itself than about the
moment of conversation devoted to it. The real relationship
is not between the novel's two characters, but between its pair

---

13. *Grass on the Wayside (Michikusa)*, translated by Edwin McClellan (revised
by J. Mehlman) (Chicago: University of Chicago Press, 1969).
14. Ibid., p. 102.

of "readers." But the latter couple will be better able to communicate if they are less constrained by the book and if it is allowed to retain its ambiguity. Such is the price paid for our inner books to have some chance, as in the distended temporality of *Groundhog Day*, of joining together for even one brief moment.

∼

We would thus be wise to avoid diminishing the books that surface in our encounters by making overly precise comments about them, but rather to welcome them in all their polyvalence. In this way, we allow none of their potential to be lost, and we open up what comes from the book—title, fragment, genuine or fake quotation, or in this case the image of the couple on a boat in Venice—to all the possibilities of connection that can be created, at that moment, between people.

This ambiguity has a certain kinship with the ambiguity of interpretation in psychoanalysis. It is because interpretation can be understood in different ways that it stands a chance of being understood by the subject to whom it is addressed, whereas if it were too clear, it might be experienced as a kind of violence against the other. And like analytic interpretation, a statement about a book is narrowly dependent on the exact moment when it is made and has meaning only in that moment.

A truly effective statement about an unread book also involves a bracketing of conscious, rational thought, a suspension that is once again reminiscent of psychoanalysis. What we are able to say about our intimate relation with a book will have more force if we have not thought about it excessively. Instead, we need only let our unconscious express itself within us and give voice, in this privileged moment of openness in language, to the secret ties that bind us to the book, and thereby to ourselves.

Letting books keep their ambiguity does not contradict the necessity to be assertive and impose your point of view on a book, as we saw in Balzac's novel. It might even be its flip side. It is a way of showing that you have grasped the specific nature of the conversational space and the singularity of each participant. Even if it is a screen book that each person is discussing, it is better not to shatter the common space, but instead to leave our phantom books intact, along with our potential to non-read and to dream.

$\approx$

Given these circumstances, one might well conclude that ultimately I invented nothing when I decided earlier in this book to save the library in *The Name of the Rose* from the flames, to unite Rollo Martins and Harry Lime's girlfriend, or to drive David Lodge's unhappy hero to suicide. To be sure, these facts are not directly stated in the texts. But like all the facts I have offered the reader in the works I have discussed, they correspond for me to what I see as the likely logic of each text and thus, as far as I'm concerned, are an integral part of them.

No doubt I will be reproached, as was the artist with gold-rimmed spectacles, for talking about books I haven't read, or

for recounting events that, literally speaking, are not part of
the books. However, it felt to me not as if I were lying, but
rather that I was uttering a subjective truth by describing
with the greatest possible accuracy what I had perceived of
these books, being faithful to myself at the moment and in
the circumstances when I felt the need to invoke them.

Speaking About Yourself

(in which we conclude, along with Oscar Wilde,
that the appropriate time span for reading a book
is ten minutes, after which you risk forgetting
that the encounter is primarily a pretext
for writing your autobiography)

AS WE SEE, the obligation to talk about unread books should not be experienced as something negative, a source of anxiety or remorse. To the person who knows how to experience it as positive, who manages to lift the burden of his guilt and pay attention to the potential of the concrete situation in which he finds himself, talking about unread books invites us into a realm of authentic creativity. We should learn to welcome the opportunity to enter this virtual library and embrace all its rich possibility.

That, in any event, is the major lesson to be drawn from Oscar Wilde's writings on the subject. These texts concentrate especially on one type of situation in which we may be led to talk about books we haven't read—that of literary criticism—but his suggestions may easily be extended to other situations, such as dialogues in social or academic settings.

~

A voracious reader if ever there was one and a man of vast culture, Oscar Wilde was also a resolute non-reader. Long before Musil or Valéry, Wilde had the courage to warn of the dangers of reading for the cultivated individual.

One of Wilde's most important contributions to the study of non-reading, because of the new channels it opens up, appeared in an article called "To read, or not to read"[1] in the *Pall Mall Gazette*, a newspaper for which he wrote regularly. Responding to an inquiry about the hundred best books it was possible to recommend, Wilde proposed dividing the contents of the collective library into three categories.

The first would consist of books to be read, a category in which Wilde places Cicero's letters, Suetonius, Vasari's lives of the painters,[2] Benvenuto Cellini's autobiography,[3] John Mandeville, Marco Polo, Saint-Simon's memoirs,[4] Mommsen, and Grote's history of Greece.[5] The second category, equally expected, would comprise books worth rereading, such as Plato and Keats. In the "sphere of poetry," Wilde adds

---

1. Oscar Wilde, *Selected Journalism* (Oxford: Oxford University Press, 2003), p. 12, UB++.
2. UB+.
3. UB+.
4. SB++.
5. UB–.

"the masters, not the minstrels"; in that of philosophy, "the seers, not the *savants.*"[6]

To these rather banal categories, Wilde adds a third that is more surprising. It consists of books it is important to dissuade the public from reading. For Wilde, such dissuasive activity is crucial and should even figure among the official missions of universities. "This mission," he notes, "is eminently needed in this age of ours, an age that reads so much that it has no time to admire, and writes so much that it has no time to think. Whoever will select out of the chaos of our modern curricula 'The Worst Hundred Books' and publish a list of them, will confer on the rising generation a real and lasting benefit."[7]

Unfortunately, Wilde did not leave us the list of the hundred books it would be important to keep away from students. However, the list is manifestly less important than the idea that reading is not always a beneficial activity, but can turn out to be harmful. So menacing is reading perceived to be that in other texts, the list of books to be proscribed seems to have been extended ad infinitum, and it is not only a hundred books that we need to be wary of, but all of them.

∾

Wilde's most important text about his wariness toward reading is called "The Critic as Artist."[8] Structured as a dialogue in two parts, it features two characters, Ernest and Gilbert. It

---

6. Wilde, op. cit., p. 12.
7. Ibid.
8. "The Critic as Artist," The Corpus of Electronic Texts Edition, http://www .ucc.ie/celt/online/E800003-007/text001.html.

is likely Gilbert who articulates the author's very original positions most trenchantly.

The first thesis developed by Gilbert is intended to counter Ernest's assertion that in the greatest artistic epochs, such as ancient Greece, there were no art critics. Refuting that statement, Gilbert cites such examples as Aristotle's *Poetics* to establish that for the Greeks, creation was inseparable from general considerations about art, and creators were thus already performing the role of critics.

This assertion serves as an introduction to a passage in which Gilbert shows how artistic creation and criticism, far from being separate activities, cannot in reality be disjoined:

> Ernest: The Greeks were, as you have pointed out, a nation of art-critics. I acknowledge it, and I feel a little sorry for them. For the creative faculty is higher than the critical. There is really no comparison between them.

> Gilbert: The antithesis between them is entirely arbitrary. Without the critical faculty, there is no artistic creation at all, worthy of the name. You spoke a little while ago of that fine spirit of choice and delicate instinct of selection by which the artist realises life for us, and gives to it a momentary perfection. Well, that spirit of choice, that subtle tact of omission, is really the critical faculty in one of its most characteristic moods, and no one who does not possess this critical faculty can create anything at all in art.[9]

---

9. Ibid., p. 121.

There is thus no separation between artistic creation and criticism, nor can there be any great creation without its share of criticism, as the example of the Greeks reveals. But the inverse is equally true, and criticism itself is a form of art:

> Ernest: You have been talking of criticism as an essential part of the creative spirit, and I now fully accept your theory. But what of criticism outside creation? I have a foolish habit of reading periodicals, and it seems to me that most modern criticism is perfectly valueless.[10]

Defending critics against this accusation of insignificance, Gilbert asserts that they are far more cultured than the authors they review, and that criticism demands infinitely more culture than artistic creation. In this defense of criticism as an art, an apologia for non-reading first appears:

> The poor reviewers are apparently reduced to be the reporters of the police-court of literature, the chroniclers of the doings of the habitual criminals of art. It is sometimes said of them that they do not read all through the works they are called upon to criticise. They do not. Or at least they should not. If they did so, they would become confirmed misanthropes [. . .] Nor is it necessary. To know the vintage and quality of a wine one need not drink the whole cask. It must be perfectly easy in half an

---

10. Ibid., p. 126.

hour to say whether a book is worth anything or worth nothing. Ten minutes are really sufficient, if one has the instinct for form. Who wants to wade through a dull volume? One tastes it, and that is quite enough—more than enough, I should imagine.[11]

The assertion that it takes only ten minutes to familiarize oneself with a book—or even considerably less, since Gilbert begins by assuming as a matter of course that critics don't read the books submitted to them—thus surfaces in a defense of critics, whose cultural sophistication should allow them to perceive the essence of a book quickly. The defense of non-reading thus enters the discussion as an offshoot of the inquiry into criticism; non-reading is said simply to be a *power* acquired by specialists, a particular ability to grasp what is essential. But the remainder of the text gives us to understand that non-reading is also a *duty*, and that there is a true risk for the critic in spending too much time reading the book he is to talk about. Or, if you prefer, there are more decisive factors in our encounters with books than the simple question of time.

∼

Over the rest of the text, Wilde elaborates on this articulation between art and criticism with increasing emphasis, to the point where he reveals a veritable distrust of reading.

---

11. Ibid., p. 127.

Continuing his defense of criticism, Gilbert asserts that it is more difficult to speak about a thing than to do it. He begins by taking examples from history and showing that the poets who related the exploits of the heroes of antiquity were more meritorious than the heroes. Whereas action "dies at the moment of its energy" and is "a base concession to fact, the world is made by the singer for the dreamer."[12]

Ernest retorts that in elevating the creative artist to such a height, there is a risk of proportionate abasement to the critic. In response, Gilbert returns to his theory of criticism as an art:

> Criticism is itself an art. And just as artistic creation implies the working of the critical faculty, and, indeed, without it cannot be said to exist at all, so Criticism is really creative in the highest sense of the word. Criticism is, in fact, both creative and independent.[13]

The idea of independence is crucial here, since it liberates critical activity from the secondary and devalued function, with relation to literature and art, to which it is often consigned. Instead, it confers on criticism a measure of true autonomy:

> Yes; independent. Criticism is no more to be judged by any low standard of imitation or resemblance than is the work of poet or sculptor. The critic occupies the same

---

12. Ibid., p. 133.
13. Ibid., p. 137.

relation to the work of art that he criticises as the artist
does to the visible world of form and colour, or the un-
seen world of passion and of thought. He does not even
require for the perfection of his art the finest materials.
Anything will serve his purpose.[14]

The work being critiqued can be totally lacking in interest, then, without impairing the critical exercise, since the
work is there only as a pretext:

And just as out of the sordid and sentimental amours
of the silly wife of a small country doctor in the squalid
village of Yonville-l'Abbaye, near Rouen, Gustave
Flaubert was able to create a classic, and make a masterpiece of style, so, from subjects of little or of no importance, such as the pictures in this year's Royal Academy,
or in any year's Royal Academy for that matter, Mr.
Lewis Morris's poems, M. Ohnet's novels, or the plays
of Mr. Henry Arthur Jones, the true critic can, if it be
his pleasure so to direct or waste his faculty of contem-
plation, produce work that will be flawless in beauty
and instinct with intellectual subtlety. Why not? Dull-
ness is always an irresistible temptation for brilliancy,
and stupidity is the permanent *Bestia Trionfans* that calls
wisdom from its cave. To an artist so creative as the
critic, what does subject-matter signify? No more and
no less than it does to the novelist and the painter. Like

---

14. Ibid., p. 138.

them, he can find his motives everywhere. Treatment
is the test. There is nothing that has not in it suggestion
or challenge.[15]

Among the examples given by Wilde, the most significant
is no doubt that of Flaubert, who boasted of *Madame
Bovary*[16] that he had written a "book about nothing," by
devoting his novel to the inhabitants of Yonville. Though
Flaubert's work is often called "realist," literature for him
was autonomous in relation to the world and obeyed its own
rules. Art had no need to concern itself with reality, even if it
remained present in the background, and was to find its own
coherence in itself.

If Wilde does not break the link completely between the
work and criticism, he strains it significantly by reducing the
work to its thematic nature, with the critical text then being
judged on the basis of its treatment of those themes and not
for its faithfulness. Concentrating on the thematic nature of
the object of criticism aligns this original text more closely
with art (which may also treat reality as no more than a pretext), at the same time that it asserts the superiority of criticism, which treats works of art the way art treats reality.

From this perspective, the critical text is no more *about* the
work than the novel, according to Flaubert, is about reality.
What I have attempted to call into question in this book is
this word *about*, in an effort to alleviate the guilt experienced
when it is forgotten. The ten minutes that Wilde recom-

15. Ibid.
16. SB and HB++.

mends we accord to a book are a function of setting that concept firmly aside. In doing so, we return criticism to itself—
to its solitude, that is, but also, happily, to its capacity for
invention.

~

For the critic, thus, literature or art occupy the same secondary position as nature for the writer or painter. Their function is not to serve as the object of his work, but to stimulate
him to write. For the only true object of criticism is not the
work it discusses, but itself.

To understand anything of Wilde's conception of criticism and reading is impossible without a clear view of the
location of the creative subject within it. According to Wilde,
it is the writer of criticism who occupies the foreground:

> Nay, more, I would say that the highest Criticism, being
> the purest form of personal impression, is in its way
> more creative than creation, as it has least reference to
> any standard external to itself, and is, in fact, its own rea-
> son for existing, and, as the Greeks would put it, in itself,
> and to itself, an end.[17]

Ultimately, criticism attains its ideal form when it no
longer has any relation with a work. Wilde's paradox lies
in making criticism an intransitive activity without support,

---

17. "The Critic as Artist," p. 139.

or rather in radically displacing its support. To put it another way, its object is not a work (since any work would do, just as any provincial housewife for Flaubert), but the critic himself:

> I am always amused by the silly vanity of those writers and artists of our day who seem to imagine that the primary function of the critic is to chatter about their second-rate work.[18]

Thus does criticism, having cut its ties to a work whose constraints handicapped it, end up revealing its relation to the literary genre that most emphatically foregrounds the subject, namely autobiography:

> That is what the highest criticism really is, the record of one's own soul. It is more fascinating than history, as it is concerned simply with oneself. It is more delightful than philosophy, as its subject is concrete and not abstract, real and not vague. It is the only civilised form of autobiography . . . [19]

Criticism is the record of a soul, and that soul is its deep object, not the transitory literary works that serve as supports in that quest. As for Valéry, the literary work is for Wilde a handicap, but for different reasons. For Valéry, the work itself prevents a critic from grasping the essence of literature, in relation to which the book is merely a contingent object. For Wilde,

---

18. Ibid., p. 140
19. Ibid.

the work leads away from the critic, who is in fact the raison d'être of the whole critical exercise. But for each of them, to read well is to turn away from the work.

~

Speaking about ourselves, then, is to Wilde what should be the ultimate aim of our critical activity. From this perspective, criticism should be protected at all cost from the grips of the work, which might otherwise distract it from that goal.

As a result, from Wilde's perspective, the literary work should be reduced to mere pretext ("To the critic the work of art is simply a suggestion for a new work of his own, that need not necessarily bear any obvious resemblance to the thing it criticizes"),[20] but if we're not careful, it can easily metamorphose into an obstacle. So it is not only because many modern works are of little interest that we shouldn't linger over them—the same, indeed, holds true for great works—but because an overly attentive reading, forgetful of the interests of the reader, may distance him from himself. Reflection on the self, meanwhile, is the primary justification for critical activity, and this alone can elevate criticism to the level of an art.

Keeping the work at a distance is thus a leitmotif of Wilde's thinking about reading and literary criticism. It leads him to this provocative formulation, which a large part of his work serves to illustrate: "I never read a book I must review;

---

20. Ibid., p. 146.

it prejudices you so."[21] At the same time that a book may stimulate the reader's thinking, it can also separate him from what, in him, is most original. Wilde's paradox is thus not concerned solely with bad books; it is even more valid for good ones. When you enter a book in order to critique it, you risk losing what is most yourself—to the hypothetical benefit of the book, but to your own detriment.

The paradox of reading is that the path toward ourselves passes through books, but that this must remain a passage. It is a *traversal of books* that a good reader engages in—a reader who knows that every book is the bearer of part of himself and can give him access to it, if only he has the wisdom not to end his journey there. And it is a traversal of just this type that we have observed in readers as diverse and as inspired as Valéry, Rollo Martins, or certain of my students who, when latching onto a single element from a work they know only vaguely or not at all, pursue their own reflection with no concern for anything else and thus take care not to lose sight of themselves.

If we bear in mind, in the numerous complex situations we have analyzed, that what is essential is to speak about ourselves and not about books, or to speak about ourselves by way of books (which is the only way, in all probability, to speak well about them), our perception of these situations changes strikingly. In fact, it is the many points of encounter between the work and ourselves that it is urgent to bring to the fore, on the basis of the limited available data. The title of the work, its

21. Quoted in Alberto Manguel, *A History of Reading* (New York: Viking, 1996), p. 284, HB++. This remark is also attributed to the British writer Sydney Smith (1771–1845).

place in the collective library, the nature of the person who tells us about it, the atmosphere established in the written or spoken exchange, among many other possible instances, offer alternatives to the book itself that allow us to talk about ourselves without dwelling upon the work too closely.

The work itself, meanwhile, vanishes into the discourse around it and gives way to a fleeting, hallucinatory object, a phantom book that attracts our every projection and shifts its shape with each remark we make about it. We would do well, therefore, to use this phantom book primarily to support the work we do on ourselves, drawing on its available elements to compose passages of our inner books and taking heed of those elements that reveal something intimate and irreplaceable about us. It is ourselves we should be listening to, not the "actual" book—even if it sometimes provides us momentum—and it is the writing of self that we must pursue without swerving.

The book invented in any given context will be credible if it emerges from the truth of the subject and is inscribed within the elaboration of his inner universe. If the Tiv, for example, propose a strong reading of *Hamlet*, even though Shakespeare's play would appear to be totally foreign to them, it is because they feel so deeply accused in the truth of their ancestral beliefs that they are prepared to animate the phantom book they have invented with a transitory life. In the end, we need not fear lying about the text, but only lying about ourselves.

~

Beyond all defensiveness, our discussion of unread books offers a privileged opportunity for self-discovery, akin to that of autobiography, to those who know how to seize it. In these conversations, whether written or spoken, language is liberated from its obligation to refer to the world and, through its traversal of books, can find a way to speak about what ordinarily eludes us.

Beyond the possibility of self-discovery, the discussion of unread books places us at the heart of the creative process, by leading us back to its source. To talk about unread books is to be present at the birth of the creative subject. In this inaugural moment when book and self separate, the reader, free at last from the weight of the words of others, may find the strength to invent his own text, and in that moment, he becomes a writer himself.

Epilogue

OUR ANALYSIS OF the delicate situations encountered in this book suggests that we have no other choice, in preparing to face such confrontations ourselves, than to accept a kind of evolution of our psychology. It is not enough for us simply to learn how to remain unflustered in these situations; we must profoundly transform our relationship to books.

To begin with, such an evolution implies extricating ourselves from a whole series of mostly unconscious taboos that burden our notion of books. Encouraged from our school years onward to think of books as untouchable objects, we feel guilty at the very thought of subjecting them to transformation.

It is necessary to lift these taboos to begin to truly listen to the infinitely mobile object that is a literary text. The text's mobility is enhanced whenever it participates in a conversation or a written exchange, where it is animated by the subjectivity of each reader and his dialogue with others, and to genuinely listen to it implies developing a particular sensitivity to all the possibilities that the book takes on in such circumstances.

But it is equally necessary to make this effort to change so that we can listen to ourselves, without missing the private resonances that connect us to every work and whose roots go deep in our history. The encounter with unread books will be more enriching—and sharable with others—if the person undergoing it draws his inspiration from deep within himself.

This different mode of listening to texts and to oneself again recalls what may reasonably be expected from psycho-analysis, the primary function of which is to free the patient from his inner constraints and, by the end of a journey over which he remains the sole master, to open him up to all his creative possibilities.

∾

To become a creator yourself: this is the project to which we have been brought by the observations drawn from our series of examples, and it is a project accessible only to those whose inner evolution has freed them from guilt completely.

These people know that talking about books you haven't read is an authentically creative activity, as worthy—even if it takes place more discreetly—as those that are more socially acknowledged. The attention accorded to traditional artistic practices has resulted, in fact, in a certain neglect and even misperception of those others that by their nature transpire in a kind of secrecy.

How can one deny, however, that talking about books you haven't read constitutes an authentic creative activity, making the same demands as other forms of art? Just think of all the skills it calls into play—listening to the potentialities of a work, analyzing its ever-changing context, paying attention to others and their reactions, taking charge of a gripping narrative—and you will surely find yourself convinced.

Furthermore, our new creativity may go far beyond our comments on unread books. At a higher level, any kind of creativity, whatever its object, entails a certain detachment from books. For as illustrated by Oscar Wilde, there is a kind of antinomy between reading and creating, since every reader runs the risk, lost as he is in someone else's book, of distancing himself from his personal universe. And if commentary on books one hasn't read is a kind of creation, the converse is also true: creation implies not lingering too long over books.

Becoming the creators of our own works is thus the logical and desirable extension of an apprenticeship in commenting on books we haven't read. This creativity is one step along the path to self-conquest and to our liberation from the burden of culture, which may impede the existence of those who haven't been trained in its mastery, and thus in the ability to bring life to their works.

~

If learning to talk about books you haven't read is for many people their first encounter with the demands of creation, particular responsibility lies with those who teach. Given their position and personal experience, teachers are ideally placed to advance this practice among their students.

Although students are initiated during their education into the art of reading and are even taught how to talk about books, the art of talking about books they haven't read is singularly absent from our curricula, as though no one had ever thought to question the premise that it is necessary to have read a book in order to talk about it. So why are we astonished by their distress when they are questioned on an exam about a book they don't "know" and cannot find the wherewithal to reply?

Our educational system is clearly failing to fulfill its duties of deconsecration, and as a result, our students remain unable to claim the right to invent books. Paralyzed by the respect due to texts and the prohibition against modifying them, forced to learn them by heart or to memorize what they "contain," too many students lose their capacity for escape and forbid themselves to call on their imagination in circumstances where that faculty would be extraordinarily useful.

To show them, instead, that a book is reinvented with every reading would give them the means to emerge unscathed, and even with some benefit, from a multitude of difficult situations. For knowing how to speak with finesse about something with which we are unacquainted has value far beyond the realm of books. As we have seen exemplified by numerous authors, the entirety of our culture opens up to those with the ability to cut the bonds between discourse and its object, and to speak about themselves.

The key, in the end, is to reveal to students what is truly essential: the world of their own creation. What better gift could you make to a student than to render him sensitive to the art of invention—which is to say, self-invention? All education should strive to help those receiving it to gain enough freedom in relation to works of art to themselves become writers and artists.

～

For all the reasons evoked in this book, I shall, for my part, continue, without allowing criticism to divert me from my path, to speak consistently and serenely about books I haven't read.

Were I to proceed otherwise and again join the mob of passive readers, I would feel that I was betraying myself by being unfaithful to the milieu from which I came; to the path among books I have been obliged to take in order to create; and to the duty I feel today to assist others in overcoming their fear of culture, and in daring to leave it behind to begin to write.